Insects as Pets

Other books by Paul Villiard

REPTILES AS PETS

EXOTIC FISH AS PETS

WILD MAMMALS AS PETS

THROUGH THE SEASONS WITH A CAMERA

MOTHS AND HOW TO REAR THEM

A FIRST BOOK OF JEWELRYMAKING

A FIRST BOOK OF CERAMICS

A FIRST BOOK OF LEATHERMAKING

A FIRST BOOK OF ENAMELING

A MANUAL OF VENEERING

HANDYMAN'S PLUMBING AND HEATING GUIDE

GROWING PAINS

THE PRACTICAL CANDYMAKING COOKBOOK

SHELLS — HOMES IN THE SEA

INSECTS AS PETS

Paul Villiard

With Photographs by the Author

Doubleday & Company, Inc., Garden City, New York

ISBN: 0-385-07700-9 Trade
       0-385-06423-3 Prebound
Library of Congress Catalog Card Number: 72-83603
Copyright © 1973 by Paul Villiard
Printed in the United States of America
First Edition

FOR ROBERT S. BRYANT

For his help and interest

Contents

Preface

While the keeping of insects as pets is not commonly practiced, for several centuries certain of these very interesting animals have been kept for various reasons. The Chinese kept crickets in small cages made of bamboo splints, and these captive insects were put together to fight, much the same as cockfights are held. Male crickets, during the mating season, will fight valiantly for the favors of a female, and the Chinese cricket-keepers took advantage of this fact to stage fights upon which wagers were made. Often these wagers were very large.

Almost any insect may be kept in captivity if the conditions for their well-being are met. They will quickly perish if they are not cared for. The lives of insects are sometimes so strange and wonderful that the time and trouble it takes to care for them is worth all the effort. It is only in recent years that man has come to realize that many insects heretofore thought to be pests are really beneficial to mankind, and should be protected as much as possible.

Not all of the little creatures we see are insects. Spiders are not. They are *Arachnids*. The familiar horseshoe crab we see when we go to the beaches is also an arachnid, closely related to the spider.

As a general rule, an insect can be recognized by having

six legs, and, if it is winged, usually having two pairs of wings. The body of an insect is divided into three main parts. The head, the thorax, and the abdomen. The wings are attached to the thorax, which corresponds to the chest in human beings. The abdomen carries the breathing apparatus in the form of a row of tiny holes along both sides, much like the row of portholes on a ship. These holes lead to a branching network of tubes through which oxygen is carried to the inner parts of the creature. They are called spiracles.

At the tip of the abdomen are the genetalia or mating apparatus of the insect, and, in the female, the ovipositor, if one is present in that species. Through this the female deposits her eggs in whatever situation is normal for that kind of insect. Some have enormously long ovipositors, useful for placing their eggs deeply within a protective location. Others have ovipositors so short to be almost unrecognizable as an egg-laying tube. These insects deposit their eggs on the surfaces of things — leaves, usually, or the bark of trees and shrubs.

Many insects have sharp, penetrating ovipositors. These species lay their eggs *within* the living bodies of other insects, or animals, or directly into the eggs of other species. When the eggs hatch, they find a ready source of food in the body of the host in which they were laid, and eat their way out through the living flesh of their victim.

We might say unfortunate and unwilling victim, but really we have no right to so condemn insects for using this method of laying eggs. By labeling their victims as unfortunate or unwilling we are using a human emotion or a human concept to describe the lives of other creatures, and this is one of the gravest mistakes we can possibly make in the study of the fellow beings on our planet.

When you undertake the investigation of the lives of creatures other than humans, you must realize an entirely different set of standards, and no emotions whatever. True, if humans were subjected to the forcible insertion of an egg, which on hatching ate its way through their body, killing the person in the process, we could say it was unfortunate and that the person was an unwilling host. For that matter, the wound made in the insertion of the "enemy" egg would, with our highly developed nervous system, probably prove fatal and kill us long before the egg hatched anyway. But the fact that this is one of the very common methods of reproduction for so many species of insects, leads us to believe that the nervous system of insects are so simple and rudimentary, that what to us would be a raging pain so great as to drive our minds mad with agony, is little more than a dull ache, if even that, to the insect.

An example of this is easily seen if you watch a praying mantis feed. When any insect is hunted down, it will make frantic efforts to escape *before* it is captured. As soon as it is in the clutches of its predator, however, the struggles become much less violent, and in the case of a mantis, which holds its victim securely in its front legs and calmly eats it alive, the prey furnishing the meal does not evince more than a token struggle, even as it is consumed. More, the insect remains alive until nearly the last mouthful, not dying from the terrible wounds caused by the first few chunks being torn from its body.

Gruesome? Only to a human being. The process is entirely normal to the mantis. Therefore, we have not the right to consider this behavior gruesome when studying the life history of a mantis, classifying that insect as cruel, horrible, insatiable, vicious, or by any other name which applies to one of our own emotions. Perhaps the exception would be in the word insatiable, because, certainly, even from an insect's viewpoint, mantids are insatiable in their need for food. They will eat anything they can catch, and they can catch nearly everything! Their appetite is enormous and constant, and they are continually on the prowl for new victims to satisfy that appetite.

Until very recently, all insects were considered nuisances

by most persons, and every one was killed on sight. Only those lucky ones who had some kind of armament or protection escaped the quick and ready swat of its human discoverer. Insecticides and poisons of all descriptions were sprayed and dusted and poured indiscriminately over nearly everything an insect could alight upon in the hope that the races of these creatures would be exterminated.

People were afraid of most insects. Parents instilled unholy fear into their children who would, after the lesson was driven home by an adult, run screaming from a honeybee, or a small spider whose deepest instinct is only to catch enough food to survive long enough to perpetuate her race.

This unreasoning fear can be somewhat explained, and so

Kits of "bug" catchers are sold everywhere.

excused, by the fact that people were ignorant of the lives of most of the creatures around them. Up until almost the beginning of the last generation (of which *I* am a member), only a few people spotted here and there had more than the barest inkling about animals other than the large and spectacular ones they hunted in the jungles of darkest Africa. This little bit of knowledge, confined as it was mainly to universities and some lower-grade schools, rarely found its way into the mind of the average person, who only had the superstitions and fears of the preceding generations to fall back on. It is no wonder they passed on this fear and lack of understanding to their children.

Those children are now the older persons of this generation, and we have the very great advantage over our fathers of

An even more complicated set of "bug" catchers contains a catcher and two ventilated jars for transporting your catch home.

having made enormous breakthroughs in many fields of knowledge, notably ecology and natural science. If we now continue to pass on to our children unreasoning fear and misunderstanding, then we are guilty of almost criminal negligence, because it is well withing the reach of every person alive today to gain an insight into the daily lives and requirements of his fellow inhabitants of the earth.

We know now, for example, that without insects, we as a race would hardly survive. Certainly we know that if insects were exterminated from the earth the entire pattern of natural history would change, and there would be entire blocks of life which could not survive. Not the least of these are the flowers and many plants. Then, without these plants, many animals depending upon them as food would also perish. The chain would continue, because the animals feeding on the plants are, in turn, part of the food chain for larger animals who would have to alter their feeding habits (practically an impossibility except over a period of hundreds or thousands of years), or perish. And so we are now studying carefully the results of indiscriminate use of pesticides, and turning more and more to biological control instead of devastating chemical warfare. For some species, it may be too late. For others, we have caught up our irresponsible actions in time. Let us by all means continue our work toward this aim and look more and more closely into the tiny lives or our interesting coinhabitants. You will be amazed at the fascinating things they do in the routine course of their daily living.

Paul Villiard
SAUGERTIES, NEW YORK
1973

CHAPTER ONE

What are Insects?

Probably the most frequent question asked a naturalist about insects is, how many different kinds are there? The answer amazes many persons. There are nearly 800,000 different species known, and the considered estimate of many naturalists is that the total number of species will be between eight and ten *million* species.

Someone once said that every fifth living thing on earth is a beetle. This includes every animal, every fish, every insect, every plant, tree, flower — every *living* thing. This might give you an idea as to how many different beetles there are in the world — almost 300,000 species! There are more than 15,000 species of crickets and grasshoppers; more than 30,000 species of aphids and cicadas; 5,000 kinds of dragonflies and damselflies; more than 85,000 kinds of common flies; nearly 115,000 species of butterflies and moths, and well over 100,000 kinds of wasps, bees, and ants.

These numbers will give you an idea of the vast quantities of insects there are. Actually, there are between 30 and 35 different *orders* of insects, divided further into 700 or more *families*. The families are broken down into the 800,000 different *species* mentioned before.

Insects live in every part of the earth, and under every

condition known. Some live in the fierce cold of the arctic re-
gions. Others live in the hottest of climates. Some live high in
the earth's atmosphere, while others spend their lives deep
under the ground.

Insects eat every living thing that exists on earth. There
are some that feed on the leaves of plants. Others only on the
juices of the plants which they suck up through a piercing pro-
boscis. Still others eat the wood itself, digesting the cellulose,
otherwise indigestible, with the aid of microscopic organisms
living in their digestive tracts. There are insects that eat only
the meat of other living insects. Still others eat meat in the
form of rotting carrion. Yet another kind eat only the juices
of other insects, leaving the solid matter, but sucking dry the
bodies of their prey.

This business of eating specific things is called an ecolog-
ical niche. In ordinary language, the word niche means a place
or a hole into which something will fit. In ecology, the word
really means the same thing, except it refers to the survival
habit of the creature. Any insect which eats one type of food
is said to have that particular niche, and it is this specialization
in feeding habit which keeps insects from overrunning the different locations on earth.

These locations are known under a name that is infre-
quently used except by biologists and ecologists, men who
study life and environment. This word is *biome,* and biomes
are those environmental locations in which certain kinds of
plants are dominant. Insects living mainly on the wood of trees
are most often to be found in a deciduous forest biome, while
those feeding on cacti and related plants will be found in a
desert biome.

Sometimes two different kinds of insects will be found in
one biome. This is generally due to large upsetting of the bal-
ance of that biome. As an example, a forest fire might destroy

several square miles of dense tree land. By the next year, this burned-over land will begin to sprout grass and small shrubs. Almost immediately insects living in shrubby biomes will invade the forest to settle in that changed area, and will continue to thrive there until the forest grows back, at which time the insects indigenous to the forest biome will displace the newcomers.

Insects move by every conceivable means of locomotion. They fly, crawl, burrow, wiggle, ride on other host insects, and even ride *inside* other insects. They swim on the water, or walk on the surface without ever sinking down. They even live underwater, taking a bubble of air down with them in order to breathe.

Some insects can walk even on the surface of water without sinking down.

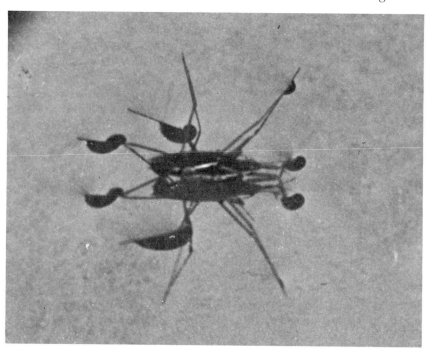

Insects breed in nearly as many ways as they move. Many insects multiply by a method called *parthenogenesis.* This means, loosely, "without a father," and in parthenogenesis, the female is capable of laying eggs which hatch into other females also capable of doing the same thing. Thus the females keep having broods of young females throughout the summer. However, when winter approaches, the female must find a male and mate with him in the manner normal to that insect. The eggs she now lays will be fertile, and will go through the winter diapause, hatching in the spring into insects which will carry on the cycle.

With these kinds of insects, the males are usually very much smaller and more insignificant than the females, and also very much rarer, seldom seen, except at the time of mating.

Other kinds of insects have the two sexes well defined, and males and females live their life span throughout the year, mating in the fall to lay eggs for overwintering.

Then there is the method known as *paedogenesis.* This name is taken from the Latin *paedo,* or *pedo,* meaning child, or son. Literally translated, the word means childbirth. Not childbirth in the sense of giving birth to a child, but rather *by* a child. In other words, these insects have one phase where they multiply by the young being born to the immature larvae. These young are really parasitic. They are born (hatched) inside the larvae and feed upon the tissues of that larvae, finally emerging from the empty skin to give birth themselves to new broods. Some mature into adults, and these mate and lay eggs to overwinter and perpetuate the species.

Some insects — the aphid is one — give birth to living young (*viviparous* reproduction) during the summer days, then mate and lay eggs in the fall which pass through the winter diapause to hatch in the spring.

Some wasps practice what is called *polyembryony,* which

Aphids live in colonies on the stems and leaves of succulent plants.

means the production of more than one embryo from one egg. In this case the female wasp lays her eggs in a host insect. Inside the host, the egg divides again and again until several hundred eggs may result. These hatch and devour the host, emerging finally as new wasps.

All of this discussion about insects and their ways is by way of giving you some information about the creatures you want to study. The more you know about anything, the easier it is to keep it in good health and creature comfort. The less you know, the more difficult it is to maintain them. If you want to observe an insect — keep it as a pet if you will — you will not keep it long unless you know what kind of insect it is, what it eats, under which kind of environment it normally lives, the temperature it must have and a few other things. The spark of life in an insect is a fragile thing, and it will quickly succumb to improper conditions.

Suppose the insect you discover is a carrion eater? Are you going to be able to supply rotting meat for its survival? Consider one of the so-called goat moths — named because the caterpillars smell to high heaven — and which feed only on *living* tree wood, boring tunnels through the trunks of the trees. Can you provide this food for your captive? Or, again, take an insect which feeds only on one species of insect. Will you be able to provide a continuing supply of food for your charge?

Keeping specific feeders is not like keeping a dog or a cat, or even any of dozens of other animals who can be fed on a variety of foods obtainable in the wintertime as well as during the summer. All of these things must be taken under consideration when deciding to keep an insect as a pet. If you do not know about the subject before you get it, the chances are you will not have time to learn it *after* you catch it, since the creature will not survive long enough for you to learn.

At best, the lives of most insects is short — one year or a

little less from hatching to death. Usually the diapause is in the egg. This is to say that the insect lays her eggs in the fall, and the eggs overwinter, hatching in the spring when food is available. The insect grows to maturity during the summer, mating and laying eggs again in the fall, then dying. A very few insects will hibernate over the winter, awakening once again in the spring, but these are the exceptions to the rule.

Some tropical insects may also be kept through the winter, provided food is available. Since these creatures live in a part of the world where killing cold is unknown and the plant life does not die off in the winter season, but remains green and succulent all year, the insects are multibrooded, or continuously brooded. One such insect is the lovely moth from India called *Actias selene,* or Indian Moon Moth. The larvae of this creature feed upon rhododendron, which, in this country, remains evergreen. This enables a person to find fresh and succulent leaves to feed the caterpillars, and, as long as they are protected from the cold, and the supply of food sufficient, they will make one brood after another right through the year.

Enclosures for keeping insects may be simple and small. With a few exceptions, insects cannot escape confinement very well. That is, a cage need only be tightly closed enough to restrain the creature — it need not be massive in strength. A few insects could eat their way out of a cage sealed with paper or cloth. Some could, if given enough time, eat their way through thin wooden cages, but, for the most part, any simple container which is large enough to provide room to move about, and has some method of admitting air, is fine for your captive. Support of some kind should also be provided, either in the form of a twig or two, some leaves, sand, or pebbles for those insects living in that kind of environment.

The thing to keep in mind, if you want to observe the life of an insect, is not to practice the "bug-in-a-bottle" method of keeping them, but to make some effort to satisfy the needs of the creature for security, creature comfort, temperature control and feeding requirements.

Before you start keeping insects, you should first decide just *why* you want to keep them. There are several reasons. One is for scientific study — if you want to discover everything you can about the behavior of a certain species, its life history, mating habits, and the various stages in the development of the creature if it is one of the metamorphic kinds (that is, if its different stages are in different shapes, changing each stage until the final adult shape is attained).

Or an insect can be used as a photographic model. Pictures can be taken of the different poses and movements of a species. In this case you need not try to set up a complete condition, or ecosystem, since you would be working with several specimens of the same insect one at a time, taking pictures as you found the opportunity, then releasing that captive to obtain a new one later.

And insects can be just "pets." It is so interesting to watch these tiny creatures go about their daily lives.

You would go about keeping the subjects in a different way for each different purpose. Let us consider the photographic angle. To photograph an insect, you must first have a "model throne" of some kind. For human beings such a "throne" is a chair, or a couch, or some piece of furniture with an appropriate background. Lights are distributed all around to kill shadows and to evenly illuminate the entire stage.

The idea is exactly the same when photographing an insect, except, as a matter of course, the "throne" and the accompanying background is infinitely smaller — insect-size, in fact — and the lighting is a bit different. For those insects which are sedentary and do not move about very much, or very fast when they *do* move, a small branch or twig is fine as a model sup-

The nest of the paper wasp makes a good photographic subject.

If the nest is empty, it can be cut away to show the inner "apartment" construction. Make sure it is *empty* before you cut into it, though.

port. This need not be inside a cage. Naturally, the twig should be one that is normal to the insect you are working with. That is to say, if your insect lives normally on low berrybushes, it would be out of character to photograph it on a willow branch for example.

Many sedentary insects will sit in one position for hours at a time. When photographing these kinds of creatures, it is often very easy to cut the twig on which they are sitting, carry it into the house or to the location you are using as your photographic studio. Then you can take its picture as many times as you wish, and return the twig to the place you got it, still with the insect not having moved.

Most insects, however, are not this co-operative, and some of them are very difficult even to approach before they take alarm and flee according to their method of locomotion. Others have very ingenious hiding tricks. These creatures naturally cannot be kept on an unconfined twig while you work with them. You will have to have a cage, preferably with a very clear, clean, flawless sheet of glass on at least one side, through which you may take the photographs. If your support is near the glass, you will be able to get the lens of your camera up close enough to take close-up pictures through a portrait lens or adapter.

Leaf hoppers are particularly cagey and interesting little creatures to photograph. They sit near the edge of a leaf until you approach too closely for their comfort. Then, with a little crablike sidestep, they skid over to the edge of the leaf and disappear around to the other side. This movement will be repeated several times before the insect takes alarm enough to flee the leaf entirely. The habit of ducking under the leaf may be used in photographing them. Simply focus your lens on the top of the leaf where the insect was sitting, then, just as you are ready to take the picture, pass your hand down under the

The leaf hopper is interesting to photograph.

leaf — not touching the leaf, but so the insect can see your hand approaching. Instantly it will pop into sight around the edge, fleeing the intruding hand, and click goes your camera shutter.

Flying insects must be caught and put inside escape-proof cages equipped with a twig support, then you simply wait until one lands in a good position for you to take its picture. Patience is 90 percent of insect photography, and you may wait almost an entire day at the cage with your camera before you get what you want.

No provisions for feeding or watering these photographic

subjects is necessary, since, as mentioned earlier, they will be released as soon as you have finished with them. For the same reason, you need not know too much about their life histories, since you are not attempting to maintain them for any length of time.

For the study of their life histories, you must go about keeping your charges in an entirely different manner. Here you will have to know at least the beginnings of their requirements — such as food, conditions under which they normally live, and temperature range. Unless you can meet these simple needs, you will be unsuccessful in keeping the insect for very long.

You must remember that the life spark in these tiny creatures is feeble at the very best, and they succumb in a day or two, in a few hours, or even in a few minutes, if these requirements are not met. Social insects such as ants and bees seem to be the easiest ones to keep in some sort of contentment. All you need is soil or sand and a handful of ants to have them immediately begin the construction of a new nest to take the place of the one from which you took them. If you have some eggs with the ants, the nest will become operative even sooner. Bees, placed within a suitable compartmented box will go about building a new hive, provided they have a queen with them.

Insects, like the different ant lions, are easily satisfied with a tray of sand, kept very slightly warm by placing it in a location where it will receive some sunlight each day. In this tray the industrious creatures will quickly build funnel traps and commence life anew after being dug out of their natural environment.

While the ant lion will remain quite contentedly in its uncovered tray, the insects used to feed it are another matter. For this reason, the tray must be placed within an escape-proof cage.

The mandibles of the larval ant lion are extended and open — ready to seize an unwary victim.

Flying insects must have cages large enough to permit constant flight, as well as a place to land, while at the same time concealment devices must be provided. In the case of very small flying insects like fruit flies, the cage can be fairly small, since the unhampered flight line of a fruit fly is a short one.

The life histories of some insects simply cannot be studied in captivity because their habits and requirements are such that you cannot provide the natural conditions under which they live their lives. These insects, therefore, should not be used for other than casual photo studies, then released as soon as you have finished with them. I can give one example — there are many — of such an insect to illustrate my point.

In Europe — specifically, in England — there exists a butterfly known locally as the Large Blue. The life history of this butterfly is almost unbelievable.

The Large Blue lays its eggs on the buds of an herb, and, when the tiny caterpillars hatch, they feed upon the petals of the opening flowers of this plant. As a caterpillar grows, it sheds or molts its skin, and this species molts three times as it feeds upon the herb blossoms. The periods of life between molts are called instars.

After the third instar, the caterpillar descends to the ground from the plant on which it hatched and fed, and thereafter *never eats plant food again!* On arrival on the ground, the caterpillar, still small, begins to wander about in an aimless fashion until it encounters an ant. Ants will fight to the death to protect their eggs and young.

To get back to our wanderer, when the ant approaches the caterpillar, it takes a position straddling the body of the "worm," and begins to stroke the tenth segment of the caterpillar with its antennae and feet. Within this section is a gland, which upon excitement by an ant, secretes a sweet fluid which the ant laps up eagerly.

After milking the caterpillar of its fluid, the ant picks up its willing victim and carries it to the anthill, where it places the caterpillar in one of the underground chambers of the nest. Here the butterfly larva remains, feeding upon the ant larvae *which are brought to it by the ants themselves* until it is time to pupate, which it does, still deep within the anthill.

A butterfly's first endeavor, after emerging from its pupal case, is to expand its wings to their full extent, then fan them dry. It is then free to take to the air in its final stage.

When the adult Large Blue butterfly emerges from its pupa, it does not expand its wings as is the normal procedure of butterflies. Instead it begins a laborious journey through the tunnels of the anthill until it finds its way to the outside open air. There, attaching itself to a twig or leaf it performs the expansion and drying process, then takes wing to mate and lay its eggs.

This story, so simply told in a page or two, occupied nearly the entire life of an English scientist to uncover and document. Many, many insects have life histories as unusual and as interesting as this one, but they have not all yet been discovered. Much remains to be learned about many of the insects, and much can be learned by observing them in the house. You do not need a well-equipped laboratory in order to discover new things about living creatures. Most of the knowledge we now have has been the result of amateurs observing very closely, and accurately reporting what they saw.

CHAPTER TWO

The Social Insects—Part One

A social insect is a kind of creature that lives in and maintains a society of some kind. In the case of insects, this society consists of a large number of insects living together in one community, contributing to the welfare of that community, and all working for the benefit of each other in the community.

Bees are social insects. Men have "kept" bees for a long time Apiculture is known as far back as the early Roman and Greek times, and, indeed, many ancient philosophers wrote extensively about bees.

When we say we keep bees, that is not exactly the way it is. True, we keep the hives, and do some little protecting of them, especially during the cold winter months, but in no sense do we actually *keep* bees. Bees keep themselves, going about their appointed tasks with no help, and, hopefully, with no hindrance from mankind. All we can do is to help them in the case of hive establishment and reap some reward by the theft of part of the honey manufactured, whether or not the bees are "willing" to part with it.

Bees may not easily be kept indoors, except in observation hives, or under laboratory conditions. These are insect pets that must be left to their own devices, and all you are able to do is to study their lives and get some honey from them. The

The group of hives here is the start of a nice apiary. The one on the left is single, the one in the middle has one super added, and the one on the right has two supers.

life of the honeybee is one of the most elaborate and fascinating in all insectdom. Many scientists have devoted their entire lives to its study, and much has been learned about the insects

However, much of what has been learned is conjecture, since we cannot be certain that our interpretations are correct. It is extremely difficult to avoid *anthropomorphism* when dealing with creatures other than man. Anthropomorphism is the attribution of human traits or emotions to animals or things. Thus, we cannot say with assurance that an animal is happy. We cannot know when or if it is happy or not.

We can judge it to be *contented* if it shows few or no signs of distress, restlessness, or other upset. But even here we cannot be sure, because what we think is contentment, or satisfaction with its treatment or surroundings, may simply be such a state of frustration that the animal has lapsed into lethargy and no longer cares about anything, lying about listlessly and making no attempt to resent handling, thus being thought of as content. And with this observation we may also be making a great mistake, since we cannot with truth say that the animal is even capable of being frustrated or aware that it is in such artificial surroundings that it loses all initiative and becomes lethargic.

The point of all this discussion is that, as I said, much has been "learned" about bees — particularly honeybees, and we believe we are right simply because of repetition on the part of the bee under certain stimulus and our interpretation of these responses.

Aristotle and Pliny wrote about bees, and students and scientists have been writing about them ever since. An Austrian scientist named Karl von Frisch perhaps delved more deeply into the life history of the honeybee than anyone else. His book on bees remains the definitive work to date. It was Von Frisch who discovered the "language" of honeybees, and who interpreted it — at least to man's satisfaction.

Through years of careful and accurate observation, repeated time after time, he proved that under one condition the behavior of a bee was always the same. Under another condition a different form of behavior was observed. Von Frisch learned these different behaviors to the point where he could document them and permit others to know what the bees were "saying" to each other. This bee communication is in the form of a dance. The bees perform this dance to indicate to other members of the hive the distance and direction of a source of pollen, and, according to Von Frisch, this communication is extremely accurate and capable of being learned by man.

Unlike the earthbound ants which do not travel through

the air and which can and do leave trails of scent by which other ants are able to locate a source of food and help carry it to the nest, bees must be able some way to direct the activities of their fellow gatherers to the field, tree, or meadow where they have located a rich source of pollen. The dance does this.

Bees are very intelligent insects and have many habits that are amazing when first learned. While there are thousands of different species of bees and wasps, we are concerned in this book with only one bee, the honeybee. Most of the bees are solitary insects, and, while some of them afford an excellent subject for study, the honeybee is the one best suited for keeping in captivity.

The hive is divided into several castes of inhabitants. First, and, of course, most important to the continuation of the hive is the queen. More about her later. Then we have the worker bees. These are unproductive females. Next are the drones,

One bee is performing her "dance" at the entrance to the hive. She seems to be communicating to her fellow workers a new source of pollen.

which do little work in the hive. The drones are males, and their main function is to mate with young queens when mating time arrives. Drones do have one other duty, especially in the summertime when the interior of the hive may reach too high temperatures, and this is to fan the hive to keep it cool. The drones cling to the sides of the hive, and by vigorously fanning their wings, create a circulation of air throughout the hive, cooling the otherwise dangerously hot interior.

The queen has but one duty, and that is to lay eggs. This duty she is perfectly designed to do. She is larger than the drones or workers, and is entirely dependent upon the other members of the hive. They feed her, clean her, tend her eggs, and perform all the natural functions of care for their queen.

A most interesting fact about bees is that you can remove the queen from a hive, and, together with a few workers and drones, set up a new hive. The old hive from which the queen was taken — kidnaped, or bee-naped, if you prefer — will, in the matter of a few hours, set about making a new queen. That they can do this is astonishing. It is done with food.

Bees use two different kinds of food. Royal jelly, about which much misinformation has been written, especially in the cosmetic field, and bee bread. Royal jelly is a substance that is secreted by special glands in the worker bees' bodies. Bee bread is a mixture of honey and pollen. All the bee larvae are fed on royal jelly for the first three days of life. Then the food is changed to bee bread, and the larvae develop into worker females.

However, if a larva is fed royal jelly continuously for its entire life, it does not develop into a worker, but into a queen instead. So if a queen is removed from a hive the bees will immediately begin to remove some cells from around a larva and feed it on royal jelly to make a new queen, capable of taking over the duties of the old queen and laying fertile eggs to perpetuate the hive.

The hive itself is made in any convenient container in the wild, or in wooden boxes in captivity. Inside the hive the bees make honeycombs or wax. These are in the form of sheets made of hexagonal cells. The bees make these cells by sticking a ring of wax to a suitable support, then shaping it into the cell by pushing the walls of the cell outward with its head. The remarkable thing about a honeycomb is the uniformity of the cells. There are two kinds of cells in a hive. The main cell is the worker cell, and this is the one in greatest profusion. The drone cells are larger than the worker cells, but there are not nearly as many of them. A thriving bee colony will contain from 35,000 to 50,000 bees, but only one queen.

When the queen becomes old, or her egg laying slows down, she is either killed or driven from the hive and the new young queens take her place. The one accepted as the queen for that hive begins her egg laying immediately. The remainder of the young queens, accompanied by many drones, fly away, mate, and form new colonies.

In artificial hives, provision must be made for the expansion of the colony, as new bees are born constantly. The average life of a busy worker is about three weeks. The queen lives about three years. In artificial hives, the main structure is a large square box with a narrow opening at the bottom of one side. It is fitted with a cover, also of wood. Inside, large sheets of comb are placed on which the bees construct their cells and fill them with eggs.

It is the habit of bees to make their honey and store it in cells at the top of the hive. Man has taken advantage of this behavior to obtain honey easily and without the destruction of the hive, which would follow if the lower part were raided for

A swarm of wild bees in a tree. At this time you can take the queen and start a new hive with part of the swarm.

You can handle swarming bees with your bare hands, since swarming bees do not ordinarily sting. Do not pinch them between your fingers.

The swarm entering a new hive after the queen has been placed inside.

A smoker. You build a fire in a can, filling it with old rags or trash — anything that will make a lot of smoke. This is blown into the hive by working the bellows.

Puff plenty of smoke down into the hive between the frames, and blow some smoke into the entrance at frequent intervals while working at the hive.

Keep the smoker going while you lift out the frame, or the bees will attack.

the honey. Boxes called supers are made to fit right on top of the main hive box. These supers are lacking both tops and bottoms, the hive itself forming the bottom, and the top of the hive fitting the top of the super. Several supers may be stacked on the top of one hive box, allowing room for a great amount of honey.

Within the super, square wooden frames, fitted with small sheets of comb material are stacked vertically, and on these the bees construct the cells and fill them with honey. It is a simple matter to remove the frames after they have been filled, substituting new frames in their place.

When taking honey from a hive, enough must be left to support the colony, or it will starve to death during the winter. For a large and thriving hive, from forty to fifty pounds of honey must be left through the winter. Since each frame holds

Some of the cells are uncapped and contain larvae nearly ready to emerge.

just about one pound of honey, it is simple arithmetic to see that from forty to fifty frames must be left in the winter hive. Of course, if the colony is smaller, a smaller portion of honey is needed for their survival. If you figure about one thousand bees to each pound of honey, you will be nearly correct in the amount.

Bees may be kept in an observation hive inside the house, if provision is made to permit free access to the outside, and further provision made to keep the bees routed into the hive entrance and not into the room. Such observation hives are readily available from companies selling study material and school supplies, or you can make one if you are handy with simple tools. Actually, an observation hive is nothing more than a regular hive with glass in two sides.

You can cut the main part out of two opposite sides of a regular hive box, fastening a sheet of glass over the opening with wooden strips or small molding. A wooden flap must be hinged at the top to close over the glass, shutting out all the light, since bees shun light in their hives. You may observe and photograph the activity going on inside the hive by lifting up a flap. Be sure to leave the flaps closed when you are not observing the creatures.

The entrance to the hive must be at a window, and a narrow board, an inch or two wide, placed under the bottom frame of the window with the frame closed down upon it (except in front of the hive entrance), will keep the bees contained. An observation hive should not be used to keep a large colony, nor for the production of honey other than the normal amount the bees make for themselves, since, in order to do this, you would have to have a stack of several supers and the base of an observation hive might not tolerate the weight.

An observation hive may even be kept in the city, or in an apartment, as long as you do not give your landlord a stroke when he finds out about it. If you live in a high apartment it would be better than one on the ground floor, because there may be too much interference in the line of travel for the bees. Bees will gather nectar and pollen from nearly any growing plant or flower. In a city hive, for example, they will gather the nectar from flowers in a nearby park, or even from window boxes along the way. Any large trees in the neighborhood, especially trees like poplar and maple, will provide a steady supply of pollen. If you live in a woodsy place in a suburban city, you may even get permission to place a few regular hives on the roof, and can keep a thriving honey business going all summer.

During the winter, hives must be protected from freezing. The easiest way to do this is to invert a larger box over the hive, filling the space between with hay or straw. Naturally, you do not cover the entrance so tightly that the bees cannot get out of the hive on warm days during the winter.

Many companies sell queen bees, if you cannot find a wild swarm and get your own. Stores like Sears Roebuck; Montgomery Ward; and other mail-order houses sell queens at certain times of the year, sending them through the mail. Or queens can be purchased from beekeepers and apiaries.

In keeping bees in captivity, no provision need be made for feeding them, since the animals obtain their own food as they provide for the hive. However, unless you are within a reasonable distance from either flowers, grasses, trees or grains, it will be difficult for the little creatures to find a ready source of sustenance for themselves.

CHAPTER THREE

The Social Insects—Part Two

Another social insect is the ant. There are a great many different kinds of ants, most of them looked upon as pests, and some
of them as household nuisances which are nearly impossible to
exterminate. Ants come in many sizes and several colors. There
are tiny red ants, tiny black ants, and even large black-and-red
ants are common. Most ants bite and their bite can be very
irritating. They produce formic acid which burns severely when
put on the skin — even more so when injected into a wound.

Despite the fact that ants are pests in the house, they are
one of the most interesting insects we can study. They are
single-minded in their work — everything for the good of the
community, and none seem to shirk their duties.

Ants are also very highly developed. They relish the sweet
nectar given off by aphids. We cannot truly say that ants have
domesticated aphids, nor even that they keep them in captivity;
still, we do know that they seem to herd aphids together, milking them regularly of the desirable fluid. They also keep other
predators away from their charges, thus performing a beneficial
service for the aphid clan.

This symbiotic relationship is one of the best-developed
ones in the insect world. Certain species of ants actually build
a "stable" for their aphid "cows," made of dirt and chewed

vegetation, inside which the aphids are placed where they can fasten their sucking tubes to the plant stem to obtain the sap on which they feed.

Certain species of ants are known to carry the eggs of aphids into their own nests to hatch. Then they carry the aphids outside to the roots and stems of suitable plants, where the sap-sucking insects fasten themselves and live out their lives, being milked of their nectar as the ants desire it.

Often, when a colony of aphids on a plant is attended by a group of ants and the plant is disturbed, each ant will immediately take an aphid in its jaws and run for safety, just the same way it will take its own egg or pupa to hide it from a marauder raiding its nest. This seems to show an awareness on the part of the ant that the aphid is something of value, and vulnerable, needing protection.

Ants are also keepers of slaves. Often you will find two species inhabiting the same nest. Usually the smaller of these species are the slaves. Slaves in ant communities may be obtained in one of two different ways. First by capture in combat or actual warfare. Next by raiding the nest of a smaller or weaker species and carrying off the eggs or pupae, hatching and rearing these in the nest of the victors. Usually the slaves seem quite contented, and do not try to escape. Actually, they have no place to escape to. The duty of the slaves is to perform the entire work of the anthill, freeing the slaveowners from this burden.

It would help to give you a short description of the anatomy of an ant, to familiarize you with your subject. A typical ant has three simple eyes and two compound eyes. The simple eyes are arranged in a triangle between the two large compound eyes. The head is large, usually with strong jaws, attached to the thorax by a short neck. The thorax and abdomen are separated by a very thin waist. Ants have the usual six legs of an insect, antennae which they use constantly as they move about, and their legs end in pincer feet, useful for traveling over uneven terrain and for holding their prey.

Some ants are blind, and these have even better developed antennae, which serve as organs of sight as well as feel and perhaps smell. The jaws of ants are double. That is, there are two sets of jaws. There are outer jaws which are used in digging, carrying food, carrying eggs or larvae and a number of other tasks. The inner jaws are for chewing, and it is these which the animal uses in feeding.

The abdomen contains two stomachs. One is really a crop, and into this goes the food when it is first swallowed. From this crop the ant can regurgitate part of the food to be eaten by other ants in the community. Some scientists call the crop the "social stomach" because it is used to share food with all other members of the colony. From the crop, part of the food is passed into the true stomach where it is digested and used for the growth and benefit of that particular ant.

The abdomen also contains poison glands. The creature does not inject this poison — formic acid — into a wound with the aid of a stinger as do bees and some wasps. Rather, the ant bites its victim, then sprays the acid into the wound. Formic acid is a powerful irritant to human skin and flesh, and the bite of an ant can be very painful, but not necessarily dangerous.

In South America, there is a species of leaf cutters — the parasol ants. These ants cut little pieces out of leaves, then carry them over their heads to their anthill. There the fragments of leaves are placed in a special chamber, and soon a species of fungus begins to grow on the vegetation. This fungus is food for the ants. Thus one may say that besides being cattle raisers, with the aphids, some ants are also farmers, rearing a crop of fungus for their food.

Their enormous capacity for biting and the bulldog ten-

dency not to let go once a good hold is obtained with the mandibles are put to good use by some South American Indians.
They use the ants to close wounds in their own bodies. If an
Indian suffers a gash or cut that is large enough to cause trouble,
he will search out a colony of leaf-cutting or parasol ants.

The wounded Indian, having found the ants, then pinches
his cut closed, and, holding the carpenter ants by the abdomen,
places them against the break in his skin. The ant immediately
bites, piercing the skin on both sides of the wound with its
large and powerful mandibles, whereupon the Indian twists
the body off the ant, leaving the head with its mandibles firmly
fixed in his skin. By placing ants at regularly spaced short intervals along the wound, the Indian effectively sews himself up.
The heads of the ants can be picked off after the wound has
healed enough to hold together by itself!

Ants are known to use themselves as seamstresses. Several
species of ants from South America, Australia, and other warm
places are aboreal, and build large nests in the trees on which
they live. These nests are made of leaves sewn together with
silk. Ants do not make silk as do spiders, caterpillars, and other
creatures. The adult ant has no spinning glands. However, their
larvae have, and they use these spinnerets for making their
cocoon in which they transform to the adult stage. During this
transformation, the spinning glands disappear, not to reappear
in the adult animal.

Since the ant must have silk in order to sew the leaves together, they ingenuously use their larvae. They grasp a mature
larva in their mandibles, and by exerting gentle pressure on its
body, cause the larva to exude a strand of silk, which the ant
uses to sew up the leaf, using the larva much as you would
use a tube of cement or glue! So we see the ant, not only working as a seamstress, but using a tool besides.

In the southwestern part of our country there are ants

which also use others of their colony for the benefit of all. These so-employed ants are called repletes, and they are used for nothing more than storage tanks for food. An ant is selected as a replete, and taken to a special chamber in the nest where it attaches itself to the roof.

Other ants in the colony now feed the replete with honey gathered from the weeds and flowers surrounding the anthill. The replete is fed so much nectar that it swells into a round globe nearly the size of a grape! Rows of repletes, hanging from the roof of the chamber, form a kind of wine cellar to which the other ants in the colony make regular trips for the purpose of drawing on their stored-up food, which the replete regurgitates when excited by stroking by its visitor.

These repletes are eaten as a delicacy by the people living where they abound. The honey they contain is considered as far superior to bee honey. In Mexico, especially, repletes are a favored delicacy, and they are regularly sold in the markets.

Ant colonies are composed of different castes of individuals, much the same as a bee colony. There is, of course, the queen. She is the founder of the colony. Under her are the worker ants. These are nonreproductive females. That is to say, while they are females, they do not mate, nor do they lay eggs. This is the sole duty of the queen, and indeed, her only duty.

There are a great many ways ant colonies are formed, and the habits of each species differ from those of other species. We can describe a "typical" method ants have of founding a new colony, with the explanation that there really isn't any typical method, only different methods.

When a colony is overburdened with individuals, or when the ants reach a certain point in maturity, a number will hatch into winged females and winged males. These two castes will swarm from the hill, sometimes in enormous numbers. The ants take flight, the females searching out the much smaller males, finally coming together, and falling to the ground where the actual mating takes place. After mating, the males die. There are, except at the time of mating and swarming, no males in an ant colony.

The female, now mated, is on the way to becoming a queen, and the first thing she may do is to divest herself of her wings. Some species bite them off their own body. Others pull them off by rubbing them against pebbles or twigs as they wander about in search for a good location to build a new nest. However they shed them, the queen is now wingless. She digs out a small nest in which to found her new colony.

Some species have the habit of carrying several special ants on their body during their mating flight. These are tiny workers whose duty it is to assist the new queen in digging out the burrow, and to feed her while she lays the first batch of eggs, since the queen will never again leave her new home.

The young queen will lay a small batch of eggs at first. These will hatch into workers who will immediately engage in the process of enlarging the nest and in foraging for food for their queen, for themselves, and for storage in the nest to feed the newcoming larvae. As the nest is enlarged, the queen lays more and more eggs which hatch into non-productive female workers. Once mated, the queen never again mates with a male, that single mating permitting her to continue laying fertile eggs for the rest of her life, which may be as long as fifteen years. The workers live only for six months or so, new ones hatching to make up the loss.

As the colony becomes better established, the workers obtain more and more food, finally getting enough to grow to their full size, and to maintain them for a much longer life than the stunted beginning workers enjoyed. The fully developed workers may live for several years, and, after from three to five years the colony will reach such size and strength, in number of inhabitants, that it will be able to hatch out a new brood of winged females and winged males to swarm in a new mating flight and establish a new colony. The old queen remains behind, not leaving the nest as does the queen bee, for example, and so the cycle begins anew.

One of the interesting aspects in the caste system practiced among the ants is the development of a large worker called the soldier ant. This ant does little work about the colony. She does not care for the queen, nor forage for food, but she does guard the hill from intruders. She is the one that does battle when an enemy approaches. She positions herself just within the entrances to the colony, often plugging the opening with her comparatively enormous head, and prohibits entry to the inner chambers.

The soldier ants are ferocious fighters, and will continue to attack and rend their opponents, even though they have had several legs amputated. The heads will continue to bite even if dismembered from the bodies. When an anthill is disturbed, it is usually the larger soldier ants you see running frantically about attacking the slightest motion, while the smaller workers are busy running to safety carrying the eggs and larvae.

While the colony lives underground, the tunnels often running for many feet in every direction, and several feet deep, the entrance and one chamber is usually under a large flat rock, a board, or sometimes even under a piece of tar paper or roofing lying on the ground. The reason for this is concealment of the entrance, but, if you lift the rock or other concealing object, the eggs and larvae are piled directly under it, numbering sometimes in the thousands. This is because the rock or board, absorbing the sunshine during the day, remains warm during the night, and makes an ideal incubator for the young of the colony. The eggs are brought up and laid out to absorb this warmth, and, when the rock is suddenly lifted, the entire

Both soldier ants and workers are frantically snatching up their cocoons to carry them to safety. The soldiers can be recognized by their larger abdomens and heads.

clutch of eggs is thus brutally exposed to danger. Hence the frantic scramble to get them back down into the safety of the nest.

Ants are found in every part of the world, in every climate and in every temperature zone. One of the reasons for their amazing success is the fact that they will eat almost anything. This adaptability also makes it easier to keep an anthill in captivity.

When deciding to keep ants, bear in mind that they will very easily escape confinement unless certain rigid precautions are taken and maintained. The old-fashioned method of keeping an anthill in an open box set in another container filled with water will work, but is subject to your own neglect and forgetfulness. Unless you examine the setup every few hours to make sure that the water in the moat is not evaporating to the point where it will no longer contain the insects, you will very quickly be infested with pests that may be very difficult to eradicate from the house.

This kind of cage is not good from another point of view. Even if you are very conscientious in the care of it, taking every precaution, you are tied to the affair. You cannot go anywhere for longer than a few hours without an "ant-sitter" available. If you want to go on a vacation trip — forget it — or get rid of your pets.

A far better system is the construction of an observation ant colony. This can easily be made by anyone who is handy with their hands and a few simple tools, and if made properly, is foolproof. The container can be made in either of two ways, the easy way, and the best way. Let's describe the easy way first. You will need two pieces of glass 10″ x 12″, and three strips of wood, two of them ½″ x ½″ x 10″ long, and the third ½″ x ½″ x 11″ long. Silicone adhesive is sold in tubes in most hardware stores, and in nearly every pet shop as aquarium sealer. Run a thin line of this along the side of the 11″ wooden strip and stick the strip to the 12″ bottom edge of one of the glass sheets. Position the strip to center it flush with the edge.

Now glue the two 10″ strips along each end of the glass, placing a layer of glue between the ends of the wooden pieces where they come together at the bottom corners to close any space that may remain between them. You should now have an assembly of a sheet of glass on which is fastened three wooden strips in the form of a "U," leaving one long edge of the glass open. Now run a line of the silicone adhesive along all the wooden strips and lay the second sheet of glass on top, pressing it into contact so the glue is continuous along the wood, leaving no gaps.

Since your ant "farm" is tall and thin, it may not stand up very steadily, so, if you like, you can cement it to a base consisting of a board about 4″ wide and 12″ to 14″ long. A good line of cement run along the bottom wooden strip will serve. Stand the case upright on the center line of the board and press it down so the cement is spread evenly under it. Prop it in position until the silicone has set, and your cage is completed, except for the cover.

This is nothing more than another narrow strip of glass which can be laid on the top of the cage. Provision for air must be made, and the easiest way to do this is to place narrow strips of adhesive tape across the top glass every inch or so, so that the glass resembles a ladder; the adhesive strips forming the rungs; with no side rails. Now the glass can be laid on the top of the cage with the adhesive strips down, leaving very thin spaces open between the strips. These will be open enough to admit air, but closed enough to prohibit the ants from crawling through.

The better way to build your cage is to use thick glass spacers instead of wooden ones. You would have to have three strips ¼″ thick glass cut, two of them 10″ long, and the last 11½″ long. These are fastened in place as were the wooden ones with a line of silicone adhesive run on the edges of the thicker glass, and the assembly is a bit different.

One end is positioned first and permitted to set. Next the bottom is fixed in place, making certain that it touches the end spacer, and that it is cemented to it. Then the last end placed in position. When all have set, the top glass can be cemented in place and the cage mounted on a wooden base as before. The same kind of top closure is used, with the narrow adhesive strips to afford entrance of air. The advantage of the all-glass cage over the one with the wooden spacers is that certain species of ants can chew their way through wood, and escape into the house, but the all-glass cage eliminates this possibility.

Whichever type of cage you use, it should be filled nearly to the top with finely sifted soil, slightly dampened, to permit it to cohere. Dry, dusty soil is not good for the purpose. The packaged loam sold in all nursery stores, most grocery stores, and many hardware stores is ideal for your ant colony. This soil — called potting soil — is clean, dampened to just the right state, and well pulverized.

Department stores, toy stores, and other establishments sell small "ant farms" made of plastic. Some of them are designed in a way that two or more may be attached to each other, making a colony of several "houses" between which the ants are permitted to travel by the attachment of plastic tubing connectors.

The disadvantages of these cages are their small size, and the fact that they provide sand for the soil in place of damp earth. The last can be overcome by merely discarding the sand

Two ant houses connected by a "runway" so the animals can travel from one farm to the other.

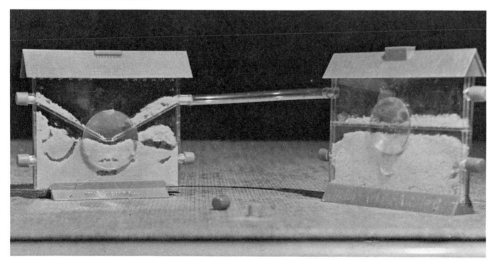

"Ant farms" are sold on blister cards, which include a certificate that you can send away for your supply of live ants.

and substituting the potting soil, but, unless you do hook up several units, your colony will have to consist of a very few members. The units are very cheap, and are usually mounted on "blister cards" as are so many items these days. With each unit is a certificate, which, upon being filled out and sent to the proper address, entitles you to a starter group of ants sent you through the mail! Feeding instructions are given, and several experiments outlined for you to follow.

Incidentally, if you live in Tennessee, South Carolina, or in Hawaii, you will have to find your own "wild" ants, since there is a federal law prohibiting the shipment of live ants in those states, nor are live ants permitted to be sent outside the continental United States.

Having set up your cage, filled it with dirt, and completed all other preparations, place the cage in the location it will occupy — not in direct sunlight, nor near or on a radiator. The ant colony will do best if maintained at ordinary room temperature, and in a shady location. Since ants normally shun sunlight, or bright daylight in their nest building, you will have to provide darkness for them to build their galleries and nests.

This is easily accomplished by fastening a sheet of black construction paper over both sides of the cage with a strip of tape at the top. This will enable you to lift the paper to observe the progress of your colony as you desire. The black paper can be left permanently in place on the back, or you can fasten both the back and the front sheets to permit viewing as you desire.

Feeding the ants is an easy matter. A few bits of rolled oats, any other cereal, bread crumbs, a small piece of fruit of almost any kind, a small bit of lettuce, celery or other vegetable, some small scraps of meat left over from your own meal, any of these placed on top of the soil will provide sustenance for the animals. One thing to avoid is overfeeding. The food will sour the soil, and probably kill the ants. Very tiny amounts of whatever you feed are all that are needed. It is a good idea to vary the diet, providing different foods from time to time, breaking up the monotony of the same food always. Birdseed is also good food, and two or three seeds are enough for a feeding, unless your colony contains hundreds or thousands of members.

The ants you will receive by sending in coupons from the purchased ant houses will only contain worker ants. No eggs or cocoons will be supplied, and no queen ants. If you collect your own, you should be able to get a good supply of cocoons and eggs along with a few dozen worker ants. These will suffice to start a thriving community. Then too, you may even be able to take a queen from an anthill, if you dig it out, looking for a very large sluggish ant in one of the deeper recesses of the colony. This would be excellent, since the colony will establish itself much more quickly with a ready-made queen than it would without one.

In any event, if you get some larvae and eggs with your ants, the first thing the ants will do is make some provision for the protection and care of these. Tunnels and galleries will be quickly dug, and the larvae and eggs stored within them.

It might be a good idea, when first introducing the animals to their new home, to have some "instant energy" ready for them. This is easily done by placing on top of the soil a teaspoonful of water, into which several drops of honey or a very small amount of sugar is dissolved, letting it soak into the ground. The ants will find the sweetness and feed on it while they are becoming acclimated to their new home.

The nest should be left undisturbed for a day or two after introducing the ants, to give them time to get their cocoons and eggs safely away. Most of the galleries will be dug up against the glass, so you should be able to readily see the inner activity of the nest quite clearly when you lift the black paper. Necessarily, some of the tunneling will be done in the dirt away from the glass, or on the back, but enough will be visible for you to observe and study the entire life history of the creatures, and to take some good photographs of them as well.

The soil should not be permitted to dry out. Each few days a teaspoon or two of water should be dribbled into the soil to soak through. At no time should you make the soil so wet as to become muddy or sopping.

Sudden jarring of the nest will cause the tunnels to collapse and ruin the work of the ants. This may even cause them to die. The nest can be carried from one place to another if you take good care not to shake or bump it during the moving.

Small bits of leaves of pear, apple, cherry, peach, plum or other fruit trees are welcome additions to the diet during the summer months. Your colony can be kept flourishing for several years if you take care of it and supply its needs.

CHAPTER FOUR

Ant Lions

A book on insects, and especially one describing how to keep ants, would hardly be complete without also telling about the ant lions. They are sometimes called "doodlebugs," but I cannot tell you how they came by that name.

The ant-lion adult is a large, winged insect that resembles a dragonfly in size and, at first glance, in shape. However, the wings of the ant lion are carried folded over the body when at rest, and they are softer and more fragile than the wings of the beautiful dragonflies. Also, the ant lion is a very poor flier as compared to the dragonfly.

The interesting thing about the ant lions is not the flying stage — the adult — but the larval stage, or the doodlebug. These creatures are voracious feeders, equipped with a strong pair of mandibles held forward on an extended appendage. They build traps in loose sand, dry dirt, thick dust, or in any medium which collapses easily. The traps are formed by the insect throwing the sand up over its body, using its forelegs and mandibles as a shovel. Soon the busy creature has hollowed out a funnel-shaped hole, at the bottom of which it buries itself, leaving only the head and mandibles sticking out in the open. It now settles down to wait for its dinner.

When a wandering insect — usually an ant — comes upon

The ant lion lurks at the bottom of its trap.

the funnel, one of several things happen. The prey may walk
over the rim of the funnel to investigate, and tumble down to
the bottom where it is immediately seized in the terrible mandibles and its juices sucked dry. The lifeless husk is then pitched
right out of the hole by the ant lion who then reburies itself in
wait for the next victim.

If the wandering insect does not fall down the funnel, but
merely wanders around the rim, the ant lion at the bottom
gathers itself ready, and when the prey is in the right position,
suddenly throws a shower of sand up in the air, knocking its
victim into the hole to seize and suck it dry.

Sometimes an insect will stumble into the funnel, but not fall clear to the bottom. Instead it attempts to scramble up the sloping sides of the trap. Again it is doomed, because the waiting ant lion delivers a barrage of sand grains like shrapnel, knocking the prey again and again to the bottom of the trap until it is knocked into position where it can be seized.

Ant lions are easy to obtain if they live in your area. They are also easy to keep until they metamorphose into the flying adult, and they are most interesting to observe. Their strength in throwing the sand up out of their traps is astonishing. After feeding, to see the shell of their prey come sailing up into the air is surprising. Soon, if you feed your pet ant lions enough,

Sift the sand into the box to remove sticks, pebbles, and other matter which would make the digging of the trap difficult for the insect.

their traps will be ringed about with the dry remains of their food.

An ant lion cage can be made of a large plastic box. You need no cover for it, since the creatures do not crawl away or fly. After the adult stage, of course, they do, and, if you wish to continue your observations past the larval stage, you should provide a screened cage into the bottom of which you can place the sandbox. Then, after metamorphosis, the adults will remain in the cage.

The plastic box should be filled with clean dry sand, sifted to loosen it well. Having made this preparation, you may go in search of your subjects. Look in dry, sunny locations, for small funnel-shaped holes in the ground. Take with you a sturdy

Look for the small funnels among dead leaves, twigs, or other debris in dry or sandy locations.

tablespoon or small sharp trowel, a large strainer, and some small containers such as pill vials. When you discover the funnels, dig a spoonful of dirt from the bottom of the funnel. Make sure you do not dig right at the bottom of the hole, or you will squash the ant lion. Rather, take a scoop of dirt out of the hole, *containing* all the dirt at the bottom, and at least an inch or two deeper than the bottom of the hole.

Dump the dirt into the strainer, and shake it to sift out the dirt. When all the grains of dirt have passed through the strainer, you should find a somewhat dizzy ant lion in the bottom. It can now be put into a collecting bottle and the cap snapped in place. Use a separate bottle for each ant lion to transport them home.

Sift the dirt, until you can find the insect, then lift it out of the strainer with a spoon — not your fingers.

Several ant lions can be placed in the same box of sand. They will separate and dig individual traps. Now you will have to feed them. This is easily done by catching almost any kind of small insect and placing them on the surface of the sand. The cover of the box will have to be used when feeding, not to keep the ant lions in, but to contain their prey, which might otherwise fly, jump, or crawl out to freedom. The insects put in for food will wander about for a time, but sooner or later they will approach one of the traps and in they tumble.

Grasshoppers, unless they are very tiny, are too strong for an ant lion to hold. Small beetles (especially soft-bodied beetles), ants, small crickets, aphids, spiders — almost any small

Several ant lions will build their traps in the same cage, at a respectable distance from each other.

creature that is not able to tear free from the doodlebug — are good food.

Toward the end of the summer the doodlebugs will make their cocoons in the sand, remaining in them until they emerge as the adult. Some species of ant lions remain in the pupal stage for two years, emerging the third year to fly and mate.

CHAPTER FIVE

Butterflies and Moths

Two of the easiest of all insects to keep, and the most fascinating in terms of life history study, are the butterfly and the moth. Some scientists make no distinction between butterflies and moths, since they are, after all, both *Lepidoptera,* or scale-winged insects. The differences are mainly biological rather than physical, but there are also a few physical differences.

Of the two, moths are far easier than butterflies to rear, since the mating procedure is far less complicated. Butterflies require flying space and usually sunshine to mate. Moths will mate on the end of a twig, or even on the end of your finger. Some moths will mate even before they have expanded their wings, and long before they have taken flight. Others require a flying time prior to the mating act.

Moths are easier to obtain for breeding purposes, too. That is, it is easier to obtain eggs for hatching. Both moths and butterflies belong to that group of insects which is said to undergo complete metamorphosis. This simply means that the insect passes through four stages in its development. Starting with the egg, the second stage is the larva. This is the familiar caterpillar one sees chewing steadily on the leaves of almost any plant, flower, tree or shrub during the summer months. Following the larva is the pupal stage, during which the insect under-

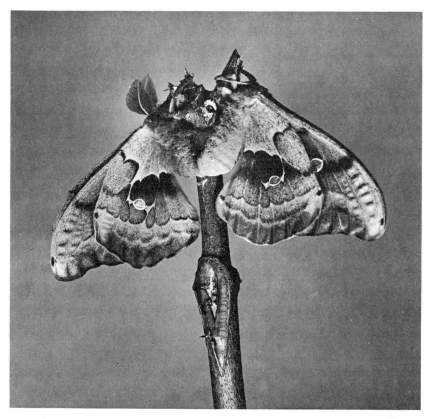

Polyphemus moths mating on a twig. Any sturdy support which will allow the female to get a good foothold will do for most of the larger silk moths.

goes a complete change of form, emerging from the pupa in its final stage as the lovely moth or beautiful butterfly.

In olden times, scientists were not aware that this metamorphosis took place, and they thought that caterpillars were a kind of "worm" and that moths and butterflies were another insect altogether. Certainly, unless a person knows the ways of transformation, the two stages do seem entirely apart from each other.

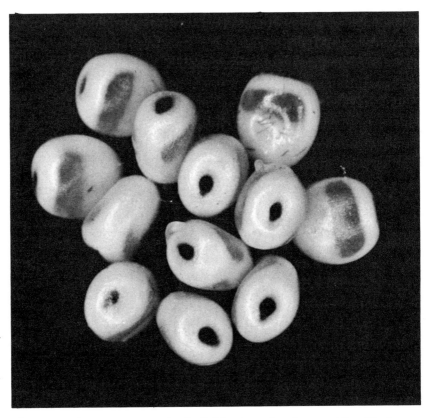

The eggs of Automeris moths look like kernels of corn. The black spot shows that the eggs are fertile.

Many butterflies, as well as many moths, do not eat in their final stage. Some sip nectar, having long, curled tongues for this purpose. Certain of the hawk moths have tongues much longer than their entire bodies, and those creatures have the ability to hover in one position in the air, dipping daintily into the tubular blossoms of flowering plants for the nectar found at the bottom. Such moths are often mistaken for tiny hummingbirds and are, indeed, called hummingbird moths because of the striking resemblance.

Fifth-instar larva. Handle them with caution.

The caterpillar spins a thin, papery cocoon that is easily damaged if your are not careful.

Automeris io has large "eye" spots on the hind wings. This is a defensive-coloration device.

Moths and butterflies are very easily reared in cages. All you need to start are eggs and the proper food plant. Most of these insects are very selective in their diet, which merely means that they eat one or two kinds of plants but refuse any other kind. Some of them are so selective that they will eat only one kind of leaf, starving to death because they cannot eat any other food. This behavior is not one of choice. One cannot say with any kind of certainty that the caterpillar does not eat a leaf because he doesn't like the taste of it. Rather, there seems to be a chemical stimulus to feed that each host plant gives off for its own species of caterpillar. Lacking this stimulus, the caterpillar simply doesn't know it is standing on food, and makes no effort to eat.

The tongue of this moth is longer than its entire body. It is able to suck the nectar from flower blossoms.

Often, if a brood of caterpillars does not begin to eat readily of food which is known to be acceptable to them, they can be started by simply trimming the edges off of the leaves, releasing the odors, sap, and other stimuli to the caterpillars, which then usually feed at once.

To obtain eggs of moths or butterflies, you can collect them in the wild, which is the best way to get them, since it teaches you not only how to find the eggs, but something of the natural life history of the insect you are studying as well. About the easiest butterfly to find is the Monarch. This familiar insect is known all over the United States. It has large rounded wings, deep reddish brown in color, with black vein markings. It lays its eggs on milkweed. In Hawaii it lives on the crown-flower.

Watch on a warm sunny day in the early summer near a stand of milkweed plants. When you see a Monarch flying around, watch her and you will see her fly to a leaf, alight for just a moment, then fly to another leaf, continuing the process all through the milkweeds. She is laying her eggs. Keep an eye on the leaf upon which she lights, then go over and examine it. Usually you will find one, sometimes more than one, tiny yellow egg attached to the underside of the leaf. Just follow the butterfly as she makes her rounds, gather the leaves as she deposits her eggs, and soon you will have your breeding stock. Pick the whole leaf — do not attempt to remove the egg or you will ruin it. The eggs are attached so tightly that you will merely break them in any attempt to remove them.

Two eggs have been fastened to the underside of this milkweed leaf. The actual size of the eggs is about the same as the head of a common pin.

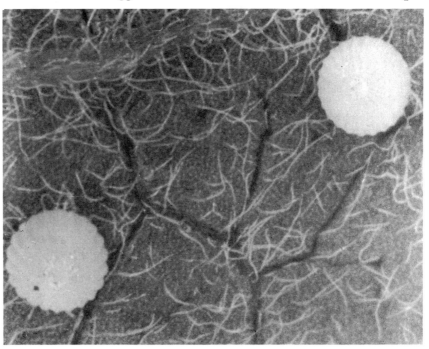

In a few days the eggs, if they are kept warm, will hatch. That is not to say that they should be heated. Just the normal outdoor temperature in the shade is fine. Lay the leaves in a plastic box which can be covered. The plastic sandwich boxes sold in nearly all supermarkets, dime stores, and variety stores are fine. Any plastic box with a tightly fitted cover will do. If the cover fits very tightly, you will have to make some provision to admit air to the eggs or they will suffocate. This can be done by inserting a strip of heavy paper under the cover when you close the box.

When the young caterpillars hatch, they will be very fragile and very small. The leaves upon which they have hatched will not be suitable for food, since they will have dried out long before the eggs hatched. As soon as you see the eggs beginning to hatch, pick a fresh leaf or two, not too many, and lay these in the box as close to the hatching caterpillars as you can without actually putting the leaves on top of the little creatures. The caterpillars should be able to find their way on the fresh leaves and begin to feed.

At first you will notice only little scratches on the surface of the leaves, since the caterpillars cannot take real bites out of their food at this time. Within a day or two, however, they will be able to actually chew bites, and you must keep fresh food available at all times.

Transferring caterpillars from stale to fresh food requires much patience and some skill. First of all, as soon as most caterpillars are disturbed, they grab the support they are on and hang on for dear life. You can actually tear the legs off some caterpillars before they will let go their tenacious grip. Some species immediately release their hold and drop to the ground, disappearing among the rubble at the base of their food tree.

The Monarch caterpillars hang on. They can be teased free with a small soft camel's-hair brush, but the best way to effect the transfer to the fresh food source is to pick up the leaf they are on, and, with a small pair of scissors, trim the leaf away from all around the little creature, leaving just enough leaf to support it. This bit of leaf, carrying the caterpillar, may now be laid on top of a fresh leaf, and the animal will walk off the old onto the new.

Within a few days the caterpillars will have grown enough to show some size. They will then stop feeding for a time and remain fixed in one position. They should never be disturbed at this time, because they are preparing to molt into their second instar. The growth of the caterpillars after molting is very rapid, and they soon reach a size where they can consume a great deal more food.

At this time the larvae may be placed in an intermediate-

The caterpillar of the Monarch butterfly is conspicuous in color. Four "horns" wave as the animal moves about, and help contribute to frightening off predators. This specimen is nearly ready to pupate.

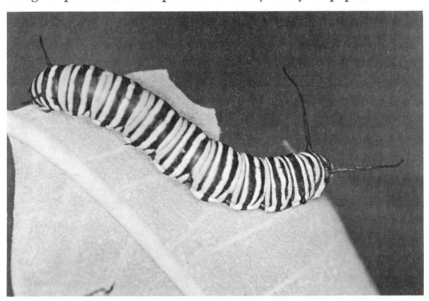

If the food plants are tall, two lamp glasses may be stacked and fastened together with masking tape. Always note the hatching date of the larvae.

sized cage. An easy one to make is a coffee-can brooder. Use a coffee can, with a hole in the lid for a cork, and one or two Coleman-lamp glasses. A cork with a hole in it is stuck through the lid and the sprigs of the food plant pushed through the hole, to project a couple of inches below. The can is filled with water and the lid put in place. The glasses are put on top of the lid and covered with a piece of cheesecloth held in place with a rubber band. The caterpillars will live in this kind of brooder until they reach their third instar.

Now they will require a larger cage. A very simple cage can be made out of a clean, sturdy corrugated cardboard carton. Select one that has not been mashed on the corners or sides — a new carton would be preferred. It should be not less than one foot deep by eighteen inches wide, and about sixteen or eighteen inches high. In one side, cut an opening large enough to leave two inches of carton all around. Over this opening, from the inside, fasten a sheet of glass with wide adhesive tape. The adhesive masking tape in office-supply companies, hardware, and variety stores will do as well as the cloth surgical adhesive tape. The main thing is to make sure the glass is held tightly all around against the sides of the carton.

Now cut a hole about one inch in diameter in the bottom of the carton. The use of this will be explained later. A second sheet of glass large enough to cover the top of the carton can be used to close the cage. You must make sure that the top edges are level so the glass closes all around. The carton should be set on two piles of some kind, to raise it off the floor or table about one inch higher than a large glass jar. One of the jars that contains instant coffee is fine for the purpose, although any wide-mouth glass jar will do. The supports for the cage may be bricks, blocks of wood, books, anything that will support the cage without tipping and which are the proper height.

You are now ready to put the cage into use. First, to satisfy the increasing appetites of the caterpillars, you will need to pick stalks of milkweed in place of just a few leaves. Milkweed has a thick, white, milky sap that is very sticky after it gets on the hands. Also, milkweed will wilt in the time it takes you to get it home after picking it, so you will have to make a few simple but necessary preparations when you gather it. Take some matches, a sharp knife to cut the plant with, a candle, and a can or jar of water with you. If there is a lot of wind, you can also take along a small cardboard carton.

When you arrive at the place where the milkweed grows, light the candle and put it into the carton as a wind shield. Now cut a stalk of milkweed that has clean, fresh leaves on it, slicing the stem diagonally instead of straight across. Cut the lengths not more than inch or two more than the height of your

Coffee cans serve as excellent legs for this cardboard-carton cage. A sheet of window glass makes a good cover.

cage carton. As soon as you have cut the weed, hold the cut surface of the stem in the flame of the candle until it is charred, then put it into the jar of water. Do not cut too much at one time. Only one or two stalks are needed for the first feedings, until the caterpillars molt again, and again grow larger.

To use the cage, the jar you used to gauge the height on which to prop the carton should be filled nearly full with water and placed under the carton directly beneath the hole in the bottom. The stems of milkweed are now stuck through this hole into the jar of water, and *all of the space around them* carefully and completely plugged with cotton, or a paper napkin, or paper tissue of some kind, either a cleaning tissue or toilet tissue. The thing to do is to make certain that every single space around, and between the stems and the hole are plugged. If not, you will surely lose the caterpillars, since they will walk down the stems right into the water and drown themselves.

By searing the stems as you cut them, the sap is sealed into the plant and the leaves will remain fresh long enough to be eaten by the caterpillars. Fresh food must be placed in the cage each day, whether or not the old food has been entirely consumed. If the caterpillars are walking about when you change the food, they may be brushed off to the new food with a small camel's-hair watercolor brush. If the caterpillars have been sitting still for several hours they should not be disturbed, since they may be preparing to molt again, and will probably be injured when you try to brush them off.

When a caterpillar molts, it spins a small pad of silk on the leaf, fastening its claspers to the pad, thus affording an anchor from which to pull out of the skin. Tearing it loose from this pad injures the animal, which may then be unable to spin another pad and molt. It will die in its too-tight skin if this happens. The way to transfer them is to pick the leaf they are on and place it on the new stalk, propping or wedging it securely. After the caterpillar has walked onto the new food, the old leaves may be removed.

As the caterpillars grow, so do their appetites, and so does their waste. This waste is in the form of little pellets, called frass, after the German word *fressen* — to eat. The frass is dry and odorless, but it should be cleaned from the cage each day. The water in the jar below the cage should also be changed daily.

A cage such as this will serve for a brood of up to fifty

smaller caterpillars like the Monarch, or for twenty to twenty-five of the large moth caterpillars. A list of species suitable for rearing can be found at the end of this chapter.

The caterpillars will molt four or five times, then make their pupa. In the case of the Monarch, the pupa will be made right on the twigs of the food plant. The caterpillar will attach itself to a stem, then transform into a shining jade-green drop, speckled with gold and black. It will shed its skin in the process, which will fall to the bottom of the cage. About ten days after the pupa is formed, it will begin to darken, and the wings of the butterfly can be seen through the pupal skin. Soon thereafter the pupal skin will split and the butterfly will crawl out, expand and dry its wings, and take flight to seek a mate. The insects can now be liberated if desired. One or two may be kept for your collection if you are making a collection of insects for study purposes.

The jadelike pupae hang from the leaves and stems of the plants. You can see the wings forming inside the pupa.

Monarchs are one of the few butterflies which migrate. Their journey is truly amazing. They fly — these fragile little creatures — more than a thousand miles, from Canada to Florida, and on the West Coast, down to Mexico. What is more amazing, even, is that their progeny, born in the southern end of their migration route, in turn migrate back to where the parents originated. The parents die in the south.

During migration, they rest at certain points in their journey, and these points have come to be known and recognized as butterfly areas. They light on the leaves and branches of trees in the rest area in such numbers that they actually bend the branches. When you consider the virtual weightlessness of a single butterfly, try to imagine how many it must take to bend a tree branch. I have seen trees laden with not less than 50,000 to 60,000 Monarchs, resting overnight during their migratory period. These trees, tall pines, looked orange and black instead of green, the butterflies almost obscuring every needle of the tree.

Moths make either a pupa or a cocoon. If they are cocoon makers, the pupa is inside the outer covering. For the cocoon makers, no special attention is needed — they will usually make them right on the food plant. For those species which make pupae, you will have to provide a box filled with clean sifted soil, kept very slightly damp for them to use. The caterpillars will dig down into the dirt and there hollow out a space within which they will pupate.

While it is best to leave the pupae undisturbed through the winter in the dirt, kept in a cool place, you can, if you wish, dig them out very gently and examine them, rolling them up in a piece of paper towel and storing them in a box over the winter. In either case, you cannot let the pupae dry out or the moth forming inside will dessicate (dry up) and die. On the other hand, they cannot be kept sopping wet, or they will drown. The soil or the paper must be kept just damp. The

Monarch butterflies alighting on their migration trees in Pacific Grove,
California. By night, these trees will be a blaze of color, entirely hidden
by the insects.

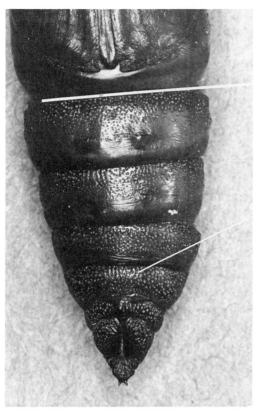
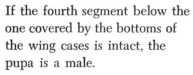
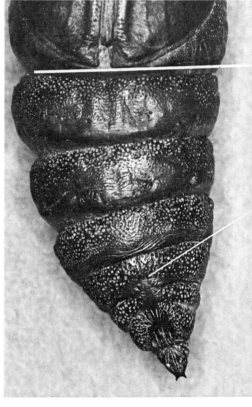

If the fourth segment below the one covered by the bottoms of the wing cases is intact, the pupa is a male.

If the fourth segment below the one covered by the bottoms of the wing cases is notched, lined, or broken in any way, the pupa is a female.

moths will pass the winter in the pupa or cocoon, emerging in the spring to mate and lay eggs.

This overwintering is called the diapause of the insect. Some moths, and some butterflies, too, diapause in the egg stage. Some do this as caterpillars, not fully grown, and a few as the adult, hibernating in sheltered places, to take wing once again in the spring.

When moth caterpillars are ready to pupate, they evacuate their gut with a large spot of liquid frass. Then they usually begin to wander restlessly about their cage. When you see them doing this, you can pick them up and place them on the dirt in the pupating box. Make no attempt to bury them. They will do this themselves. Do not disturb them for at least a week after they dig down out of sight. You may kill them if you expose them in the pupal stage. The soil in the pupating box may be the sifted potting soil bought in small sacks in grocery stores, supermarkets, and nurseries.

Moth eggs may be obtained by trapping a live female moth and placing her in a large paper sack, closed by folding the top several times and putting a paper clip over the folds. She will lay her eggs on the paper, which may then be cut out of the sack and treated as though it were a leaf with the eggs upon it. The hatching and rearing is the same for almost every species of moth or butterfly. Some vary, but these are rare and exotic species which you should not be able to obtain anyway.

To trap wild moths, a light placed outdoors at night with a white cloth supported behind it should work. A "black" light works even better. The moths are attracted to the light and land on the white sheet, where they may be captured and placed in a bag.

The females have much thinner antennae than the males, and fatter and larger bodies. The eggs of moths — and some butterflies — may also be purchased from breeders throughout the country and abroad. It is useless to order butterfly eggs from foreign breeders, since butterfly eggs hatch so rapidly they cannot tolerate the trip through the mails. They will invariably be hatched and dead on arrival.

Moth eggs, on the other hand, take ten days or more to hatch, and can stand the joggling and vibration of an airmail trip. Unless you know the proper food plant for the caterpillars, and, even more importantly, unless you have a ready *source* of that food plant, don't order the eggs. If you do not know the food plant, be sure to tell the breeder you order from to include the name of the foods required with the eggs. All breeders will do this, willingly.

An excellent collection of perfect specimens of moths and butterflies may be made by rearing them yourself. As soon as the wings have expanded and dried, the specimen can be killed and mounted. You can find books on how to do this in any library, or your science teacher at school can tell you, and even help you, if he knows you are serious about learning to do it. In Chapter Fourteen there are a few directions for mounting your butterfly and moth specimens, and also how to keep other kinds of insects.

Some of the species which you could rear successfully in cages are listed here for your convenience, together with the food plants they require.

Antheraea pernyi	oak, apple.
Antheraea yamamai	oak, apple, chestnut, hickory, plum.
Attacus atlas	lilac, cherry, privet, sassafras.
Automeris io	cherry, lilac, privet, poplar, elm.
Bombyx mori	mulberry.
Callosamia promethia	cherry, lilac, privet, spicebush, willow.
Celerio lineata	grape, Virginia creeper.
Estigmene acraea	oleander, sea grape, or almost any low weed.
Hemileuca maia	willow, oak, cherry, poplar.
Rothschildia jacobaea	privet.
Rothschildia orizaba	privet, lilac, willow, cherry, and others.

| *Hyalphora cecropia* | cherry, willow, lilac, apple. |
| *Telea polyphemus* | oak, chestnut, cherry, willow. |

Not all the food plants accepted are listed for all the species named above, but enough are so you should have no trouble finding a proper plant. Also, there are many more species that can be reared, but I have just listed a few to get you started. A few names and addresses of breeders who sell eggs and cocoons are also listed here. The breeders in this country can send you cocoons. Those in foreign countries will send only eggs.

Robert S. Bryant, 522 Old Orchard Road, Baltimore, Maryland 21229

Paul W. Beard, 17 Cielo Vista Terrace, Monterey, California 93940

Duke Downey, Box 558, Sheridan, Wyoming 82801

Otto Jancik, Furth-Gottweig, 80 N.O. Austria

Thomas R. Tewksbury, 69 Riverside Avenue, Massapequa, New York 11758

Worldwide Butterflies Ltd., Over Compton, Sherborne, Dorset, England.

When writing for information or price lists, it is only courtesy that you enclose a stamped, addressed envelope for their reply. Your letter may not mean a lot to you, but when you consider the amount of mail these persons receive their postage bill is alarming, so always send a stamp.

CHAPTER SIX

The Mantis

Of all the insects that can be kept in captivity, I like best the great *Mantis religiosa* — the praying mantis. I must mention before I go much further that the mantis is a protected insect, and it is against the law to kill them or otherwise harm them. Mantids can turn their heads to look over their shoulder, or to watch their prey, or you. They can make you very uncomfortable with their inscrutable stare because their eyes have a tiny black pupil deep within them.

The life of a mantis is an interesting one. They hatch from eggs contained in a hardened froth which the female places on a suitable support in the early fall or late summer, and which can withstand the rigors of freezing winter days and nights with no harm to the eggs. Several hundred eggs are laid in each *ootheca* (as the egg cases of the mantis are called). When the young hatch, they boil out of the case, hanging festooned from it. Finally dropping to the ground, the young scamper off in all directions, since, besides eating everything that moves, mantids also eat each other! They have ravenous appetites.

While one or two may stay together, a wary distance from each other, for the most part they are solitary insects, each going about its own way. As they grow, most of them are eaten by others of the colony, and this is one way of keeping the mantis population under control. When mating time arrives, the males literally take their lives in their own hands in the attempt to find a mate.

As a male discovers a female and approaches her, there is a better chance that he will be caught and eaten alive, than that he will mate with her. Sometimes a female will consume several males before she permits one to mate her. Even then he is not safe, because most generally, as soon as the mating act is completed, the female calmly reaches over her shoulder to

When the mating is over, the chances are that the male will be eaten by his mate.

grasp the male in her strong front legs, brings him around to the front where she can conveniently reach him, and proceeds to eat him alive like an ear of corn, chewing her way from one end to the other.

A few weeks after mating the female will begin to grow to an enormous size. That is her body will grow large. She is filling up with eggs. When she looks as though she is going to pop she will find a place on the stem of a plant; in a corner of the cage, if you have her caged; on the drapes at a window; and begin to extrude her frothy ootheca. As it is made, the froth is white and soft. The insect pushes out a bit, then pushes it into position on the support. Then she pushes out a bit more, adding it to the first. In this fashion the ootheca is built up until it is a rippled mass about 1½″ to 2″ long, and perhaps ¾″ in diameter.

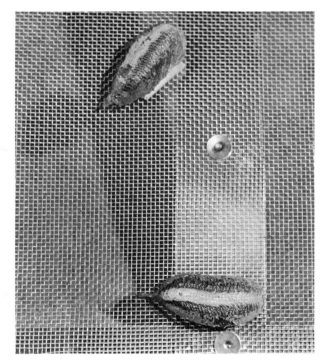

Two oothecas on the lid of a cage. These can be peeled off or left in place to overwinter, but they should be placed outdoors to freeze and thaw through the season.

Shortly after being made, the froth hardens and the case is all ready to overwinter.

There are large number of species of mantids. Some of them from exotic lands are absolutely beautiful, looking like the blossoms of rare and unusual flowers. One in particular, is a delicate pink, flushed with deeper rose, and is almost impossible to detect on the flower on which it habitually makes its home.

Some mantids are quite small. One we have in this country, which is an alien, by the way, having been imported from China many years ago, is a medium-sized insect. Females will reach nearly 5″ in length if they find enough food and survive long enough. Males are smaller, and the bodies of the males are narrower than those of the females. Some specimens are brown and some are green. Both brown and green ones can come out of the same batch of eggs. We have several other species, but the Chinese mantis is the most common in the east.

The praying mantis comes nearest of all the insects to being a pet. It can be permitted freedom in the house, which it will soon clear of every other bug or insect. It is clean and neat, washing its face and feet many times each day, very much like a cat washes and grooms its body. After the insect has become used to you, it will take food from your fingers, resting on your hand or perched on a fingertip while it dines. It will eat any kind of insect, provided the insect is alive and moving. Still prey seems not to be desired. This is perhaps because the unmoving insect does not attract the attention of the mantis, and the latter cannot see it, or does not recognize it as food.

Move it a bit, though, and it will be snatched up in the long, toothed, powerful front legs. Once caught in these wonderful pincers, the prey has little chance of escaping. Very seldom does a mantis lose an insect once it has it in its grip. While the prey is alive and kicking, the mantis eats it completely, except for the hard chitin outer shell and the wings. These drop to the ground as they are pulled free of the body. The mantis is so fast and so accurate with its catching-feet that it can pick flies out of the air as they zip by. The appetite of a mantis seems never to be satisfied. It feeds almost continually through the day. Beetles, bees, ants, wasps, butterflies, flies, all are so much food for your pet.

One specimen I kept for a long time would take and eat mealworms from my fingers, consuming them with evident relish, but would rarely take them if they were placed free. This because the mealworm is not an active insect, but crawls so very slowly that its motion does not attract the attention of the mantis. When held by the end in the fingers, however, mealworms twist and turn trying to free themselves, and, if the twisting worm is held up in front of the mantis, it is readily accepted.

After the egg case is made, the mantis dies in a short time. By the time cold weather sets in, all the adults are gone, and the young hatching the next spring never know or see their parents. They would have, of course, no chance to see their father in any event, who would long since have been digested by the mother. A most inaccurate, but amusing cartoon was recently printed, showing a few small mantids sitting in a circle about a large one. The caption read, "Mommy, tell us again that bit about how you ate Daddy!"

All you need to keep a mantis for study is a large glass jar with a wide screw cap, into which you punch several holes. Punch the holes from the inside out so the sharp points of metal do not injure the captive. Into the jar place a branchy twig to afford support for your pet. You can feed it by introducing live insects into the jar with the mantis, or you can let him out to roam about the room, in which case you had better hold the food insect and give it to the mantis from your fingers.

Mantids can fly quite well, although their flight is lumbering and somewhat slow compared with most insects. However, mantids fly high, and therefore are difficult to catch once they have taken alarm. If you watch where they land, you can go close enough to snatch them suddenly from the branch. They can bite, but it is a feeble thing, and not painful. They can, however, actually eat a hole in your finger if you care to stand still and let them. I suppose, if you stand and wiggle your finger while they chew at it, they will eat it all, leaving the nail and the bones. So far, I haven't found anyone who wants to try that experiment.

A word of caution. If you keep a mantis, or a pair of them, and they mate and the female makes her ootheca in the house, remove it from the support by carefully peeling it away, and keep it in a large container outdoors, or in a cage indoors. Otherwise, on some unsuspected day in the spring you will be deep in tiny scampering mantids who will run over the entire house. True, they don't hurt anything, or you, but the other members of your family may not appreciate several hundred hungry little insects searching out every thing that moves in order to eat it.

CHAPTER SEVEN

The Walkingstick

Related to the mantis is the walkingstick — a truly weird creature found clinging to twigs and branches low to the ground, or in trees, where they feed upon the leaves. Stick insects are *parthenogenetic,* and males are very rare. They feed upon plants, and some species can be reared in cages. The only difficulty is finding them to begin with, because unless you just happen to look directly at one from a very short distance, it will be invisible to the human eye — invisible to the eye of its enemy too, hopefully. About the only time you manage to see one in the wild is when it moves as you pass by and the motion attracts your vision.

Some of the larger insect breeders, especially those in Europe and England, offer eggs of the giant walkingstick for sale. These can be purchased and hatched in the home. They come from Africa.

An aquarium with sand or soil on the bottom, and branchy twigs for the insect to walk on are all that is necessary to house walkingsticks. Water can be sprinkled on the twigs each day, or two times daily, to afford moisture and humidity for the insects. Fresh food in the form of leaves must be in constant supply, and this food must be of a kind acceptable to the creature.

Just because they eat leaves does not mean that they will

eat any old kind of leaf you happen to put before them. It is usually safe to assume that the leaves of the plant or tree you found them on are at least one type of food the insect will eat. At any rate, try them and see if they are eaten.

Try, also, a variety of different leaves, watching to see which are accepted and which are not. The common stick insect found in the North will feed readily on willow, locust, and privet. They may take a variety of other kinds of leaves as well. The giant African walkingstick (whose eggs are sold by Worldwide Butterflies Ltd., at the address given in the chapter on butterflies) feeds on privet.

Walkingsticks are harmless. They do not bite or sting. When handling them be gentle, because their enormously long legs snap off without any pressure to speak of, and break at the

Unless they move, stick insects are most difficult to see.

slightest effort. Let them walk on you, do not try to walk them or influence them other than putting a hand in their way to reroute their path.

Unless you are extremely fortunate in finding a male and a female, you will be unable to overwinter these interesting insects. The females may lay eggs which will hatch out into other females during the summer, but the eggs resulting from an actual mating of both sexes are necessary to overwinter.

Occasionally breeders in England offer the eggs of a fantastic leaf insect called *Extatosoma tiaratum* from Australia. These are related to the stick insects and are also vegetarians. They can be reared on many different leaves, and feed at night, remaining still and inconspicuous during the daytime. Sprinkle the leaves at least twice a day, in the early morning and at night. The insects will drink the "dew" drops from the leaves. Try feeding them privet, willow, cherry, pear, locust, birch and many other species of plants.

CHAPTER EIGHT

Mealworms

An insect that is not as lively or as voracious as the praying mantis, but which is easy to keep and which also serves a useful purpose of you have other pets, is the mealworm. Mealworms are a basic food for many creatures. Large tropical fish relish them. Birds eat them. Reptiles, such as turtles, small lizards, small snakes and chameleons, all thrive on a mealworm diet. Amphibians, such as frogs, toads, and salamanders, all eat mealworms, so you see, besides learning from the study of mealworm life, you can maintain a thriving grocery store for your other pets by keeping a box of these insects in the house.

Mealworms really are the larval stage of a beetle, *Tenebrio molitor*. The insect lives in dry cereals and grains, and millions of them are raised each year for pet food and for research in laboratories. A culture of mealworms is very easy to maintain. The culture shown in this chapter has been going in my home for nearly six years and shows no signs of slowing down.

A large plastic box fitted with a snug cover makes a good "farm" for mealworms. Clean burlap, cut to fit the inside of the box, is used for foothold for the insects, a place to lay the eggs, and secure shelter for the newly hatched larvae. Place a handful of almost any kind of cereal on the bottom of the box, spreading it evenly. Cream of Wheat, Wheatena, rolled oats, corn meal, any of these are good food for the *Tenebrio*. Slice a small potato very thinly, lay two or three slices on top of the cereal, and add a dozen or two mealworms, which you have purchased from your local pet shop. Ask for large worms when you buy them, since these will pupate faster than young ones, which first have to grow up.

Now cover the whole with one sheet of burlap. Again spread another handful of cereal, a few slices of potato, a few worms, and cover with a second sheet of burlap. Continue in this manner until the box is filled with five or six layers of burlap, then put on the cover and place the farm in a warm dry place.

Plastic boxes with holes cut into the lids and screens fastened over the holes make good places to raise mealworms.

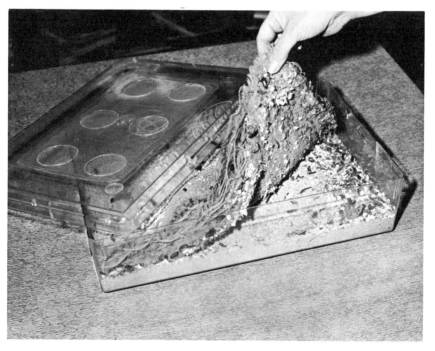

The time for the culture to start bearing worms is several weeks to a few months, depending on the age of the worms you used to start with. If they were large mature worms nearly ready to pupate, the time will be shorter. The worms make a naked pupa, remaining in this state for several days, finally metamorphosing into small dark beetles. The beetles mate and lay eggs, which again hatch into worms.

On hatching, the worms are so tiny you can hardly see them. In a few weeks they are large enough to see and can be used as food for small fishes or baby birds. Medium-sized worms are fine for larger fishes.

If you are raising mealworms for food purposes, it is a good idea to start two or even three farms, about six weeks apart. Number or mark the boxes so you will remember which is the first and so on. Then, when the farms begin to bear worms, you can feed out of the first for a couple of weeks, or even a month. Switch to the second farm after a month, to give the first a time to rest and rebuild its population. After the second month the third box can be used, and after one has been used for the appointed time, you go back to the first farm. In this way you will have a constant, uninterrupted supply of live food for your pets without exhausting any one culture of worms.

Dampness is fatal to mealworms. They cannot tolerate moisture, and care must be taken to see that moisture does not enter the boxes. This can happen by keeping the boxes too warm as well as too cool. There is the possibility of sweating *inside* the boxes, which would have the same result as if water were spilled in them. A normal room temperature is the best.

When the farms are working, and the mealworms ready for use, they can be picked out of the burlap with a pair of tweezers. Take care, if you are using them as food, that the insects do not carry threads of the burlap on their legs, since the burlap may strangle the pet you feed the worms to. In time the burlap will become chewed and pulled into a soft fuzzy mass. Then it is time to discard the burlap and start with fresh layers of cloth, dumping all the loose material into the new "farm" as well as a few new worms for fresh bloodlines. Every six weeks to two months some new cereal should be sprinkled between the layers of burlap, and a few fresh slices of potato. Apple can also be used.

There is a second method of raising mealworms, and while this method eliminates the burlap and the necessity of disentangling the worms from the fibers, I still prefer the burlap method. However, you may prefer to try the second way, so here it is. In a box, the same kind as described, place 1½″ to 2″ of meal, cereal, or a mixture of the two. Obtain a roll of the paper towels which are strengthened by a nylon web — they are advertised on television all the time — or a package of Handi-Wipes. All supermarkets sell both. The Handi-Wipes are the strongest. Unfold one and cover the cereal with it, then wet a second one, wring it out, and place on top of the first. On top of the towels place slices of potato or apple. Introducing the starter worms either by laying them on the towel or by dropping them into the cereal before covering it. All other arrangements are the same — keeping in a warm dry place, etc.

The worms are gathered by sifting them from the meal in a small tea strainer, or by raking through the meal with a fork, catching the worm in a pair of tweezers when it is uncovered. When all the cereal in either kind of culture is reduced to a fine powder, it is time to start new cultures, or add fresh cereal.

CHAPTER NINE

Fruit Flies

While we are on the subject of raising insects in cultures, for food purposes as well as study purposes, we should include fruit flies. Fruit flies — *Drosophila* — are reared in countless millions for fish food and animal food. They are also one of the most useful animals in the laboratory for experiments in many different fields. Fruit flies are used extensively in genetic experiments because they breed and mature so rapidly that many generations can be followed in a comparatively short time. This is a most valuable trait when we try to "fix" a strain of any kind.

There are many different species of *Drosophila,* both winged and wingless. As would be expected, the winged ones fly, and the wingless ones cannot fly, but merely crawl and hop about. For ease of handling, we are interested mainly in the wingless variety, and these are the subjects of our discussion in this book.

Fruit flies are marvelous food for tropical fishes and for small reptiles, particularly baby chameleons. Cultures of these interesting insects are easy to start and easy to maintain. All you need are a few large jars such as the ones instant coffee come in. The covers can be discarded, since without some special equipment it would be difficult for you to drill holes in the covers small enough to confine the flies, yet large enough to admit air. We will substitute cloth and a rubber band for the screw caps of the jars.

The first thing you must do is prepare a culture medium. This is nothing more than a nutritious mush cooked up as follows:

Water	¾ cup
Molasses	1½ tablespoons
Salt	1 pinch
Cream of Wheat	2½ tablespoons
Dry yeast	1 package

Bring the water, molasses, and the salt to a boil in a small pan. Slowly sprinkle the cereal into the boiling water, stirring constantly. Cook until the mush begins to thicken, then quickly pour into the bottoms of the jars, dividing the material equally between the jars. This recipe will make enough medium for about four jars, and these should be ready at hand before you begin to cook the cereal. Divide the yeast into four equal parts, and as soon as the mush is poured into the jars and before it hardens, sprinkle the yeast on the surface of the medium. Loosely fold up a paper towel and stick it down into the mush, cutting or tearing the paper towel to fit just under the top of the jar. Put the jars aside to permit the mush to cool, and when cool, they are ready for the inhabitants.

Ordinary fruit flies may be captured in the wild very easily. You merely put several small wide-mouthed bottles around the house with a piece of very ripe fruit — banana, peach, melon — almost any fruit that becomes soft and wet as it becomes over-ripe. In a short time you will see from two or three to several tiny fruit flies buzzing around the fruit. Simply clap your hand over the top of the trap and you have the start of your culture.

Wingless fruit flies are another matter. These are best obtained by sending an order to any of the several mail order companies who sell starting cultures. Laboratory supply houses, biological supply companies, and pet food companies all sell cultures of various insects. You can find their ads in pet magazines, tropical fish magazines, and in your school libraries. The starting cultures are cheap and are sent through the mail.

However you get your starting culture, when the jars are ready, shake a few flies into each jar and cover with a square of thin cloth held in place by snapping a rubber band around the top of the jar. The average life of a fly is about one month, and new generations are hatched about every ten days.

Fruit fly cultures are shipped in small plastic containers. They must be kept for about a week to permit the flies to mature before starting your cultures.

The containers are emptied into your culture jars as soon as the flies emerge from their cocoons. Each shipping container will make three or four culture jars at intervals of ten days or two weeks.

By making up several jars and starting cultures in them, you can keep a steady supply of fruit flies for your needs.

After you see the culture jars filling with flies — about a week to ten days after starting — you can begin using them for food. Remove the cloth cover and shake out the insects on top of the water in your fish tank, then replace the cover. Feed from alternate jars, so you do not exhaust each culture.

Once a month or every six weeks, it will be necessary to make a fresh batch of mush and start new jars. After the flies have been transferred to the new ones, the old jars can be scraped clean, washed thoroughly, and set aside to use again.

CHAPTER TEN

Crickets

In the Orient — particularly in China — people keep crickets in small cages. The most highly prized cricket in China is the graveyard cricket, said to inhabit the dry bones of long dead persons. The cricket fights mentioned in the preface of this book usually end when one cricket upsets the other, putting it on its back with all its legs waving in the air. The fights are not necessarily to the death. Crickets, like most other animals except mankind, are satisfied with overcoming their opponent, not killing it unless for food.

There are several species of crickets, and their musical chirp is a familiar sound on hot summer days and nights. Hardly a home in the country and suburban areas has not had a cricket on two chirping mightily away in the evening. Only the males sing, the females being much too busy with their egg laying to bother with cheery summer song.

An interesting thing about the common field cricket is the timing of its chirp as related to the temperature. This is so accurate that it his been documented, and a graph could be made to tell you the exact temperature of the outdoors by timing the chirps of the crickets. The formula is simple. Count the cricket's chirps for exactly 15 seconds, then, to this number, add 40. The sum of the two numbers is the temperature. Naturally, you

The bamboo cricket cages sold in oriental stores are not very practical for keeping crickets. Small ones walk right out between the bars.

must single out one particular cricket and count its chirps exclusively, not including all the different chirps that may be sounding on a summer evening.

The song of a cricket is really a stridulation caused by the vibration of the wings. On one wing a roughened vein is called the file, and on the other, a corrugated part is called the scraper. When the cricket, erecting his wings, draws the file across the scraper, the wings vibrate rapidly, causing the chirp. It has been discovered that the frequency of the cricket's stridulation is about 5,000 cycles per second.

Not all crickets chirp. First, only the winged crickets chirp at all, and not all of the winged ones do so. Three species of crickets are most commonly seen about our homes and fields. The first and most common being the black field cricket — *Gryllus*. This is the cheerful chirper heard in the summer. The black field crickets live under rocks, boards, bark or almost anything on the ground. They feed on grasses and weeds, insects, and each other.

In dark and damp cellars are found the cave or camel

This is a cave cricket — also called camel cricket. It is tan and brown, and it lives in damp cellars and caves.

crickets. These are much larger than the field cricket and stand high on very long legs. Their antennae are enormously long and thin, extending two or more times the length of their entire body. Their bodies are smooth and glossy, tan with dark brown lines. Cave crickets do not chirp.

Another kind of cricket found outdoors is the mole cricket. This one lives underground, and the front legs are greatly modified into shovel-like appendages for digging. They make long tunnels just under the roots of grass and growing plants, and they feed on these roots. The mole crickets reach a length of two inches. There are several other species.

In the western part of the country lives the Jerusalem cricket, a pretty insect of shiny yellow with dark brown stripes on the abdomen.

The diet of crickets is varied. One might almost call them omnivorous — they will eat nearly anything, including the glue from bookbindings, the wool in carpets, sizing from wallpaper, fruits, vegetables, meat, and, as I mentioned earlier, each other. For this reason crickets cannot tolerate a high population density in their cages. You must leave them plenty of room to move about in order to dodge each other, and plenty of hiding places, such as flat rocks, a branch or piece of bark laid on the dirt in the cage, twiggy branches on which they can climb.

Crickets cannot climb up a smooth glass surface, so, if you have one large enough, an old aquarium makes an ideal cage for your insects. If the walls of the aquarium are more than 12″ high — or that is, if the height of the glass is greater than 12″ from the surface of the soil in the bottom, you should not have to cover the cage, because from a standing start, crickets cannot jump up that high. However, if you have rocks, or a branch in the cage, as you should have, then a cover is necessary or the insects will walk up the branch and jump out of the aquarium.

Cannibalism may be slowed down by making sure you feed them enough, and by keeping only a very few specimens in any one cage at one time. In a 20-gallon aquarium, for example, twelve crickets would be as many as it is wise to try to keep. If the greater number of these are females, there will be

A small aquarium is a fine cricket cage, providing the accessories do not reach high enough to permit the insects from climbing up and jumping out.

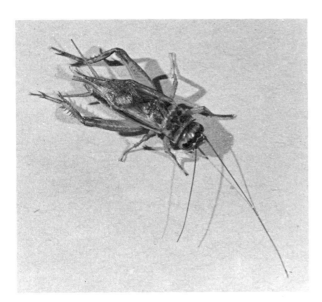

The male cricket has no central spike. There is, instead, a brushlike appendage at the end of the abdomen.

This female lost one antenna while she was being photographed. Note the long ovipositor with which she lays her eggs deep underground.

less chance of wars starting. Sexing crickets may be done at a glance. From the rear end of the abdomen, males have two long spikes, one on each side. Females have three — the one on each side and an even longer one in the center. This third appendage is her ovipositor, through which she deposits her eggs into the soil.

The rearing of crickets has become a very lucrative business, and there are a few persons in this country who rear them by the hundreds of thousands all through the year. Crickets are an excellent source of food for captive reptiles and birds, and museums and zoos use them in great quantities, usually purchasing them from cricket growers by the thousand. Selph's Cricket Ranch (P.O. Box 2123, De Soto Station, Memphis, Tennessee 38102) is one of the largest cricket raisers in the country. They send crickets via air mail to every part of the country.

Unless you feed your pets juicy fruits each day, you will have to have a supply of water for them. This is done by filling a small bottle with water, then, rolling a paper towel up very tightly, use it as a stopper, cutting off the plug at the top of the bottle, leaving just a small bit of towel sticking out of the neck. The towel will absorb the water, remaining wet. The crickets can sip the water from the paper, without drowning in the bottle. The water and towel should be changed daily.

In the fall the crickets mate and the females, driving their ovipositors into the ground, lay their eggs under the surface of the soil. The adults then die as soon as the first hard frost hits them. The eggs overwinter in the ground, emerging as tiny insects in the late spring. In the cage, your crickets will lay eggs only if the soil is slightly damp — not wet — and provided they have not been crowded. Crickets need a humid atmosphere, and if the location of the cage is very dry, it should be sprinkled inside each day to provide some humidity. Never keep a cricket cage in direct sunlight, as they live in dark or dim lighting.

CHAPTER ELEVEN

Grasshoppers

Another insect that is good food for pets is the grasshopper. While these are not as easy to keep as crickets, they may be raised if you provide proper conditions for them.

Grasshoppers, unlike crickets, can climb up sheer surfaces, so you will have to keep their cage covered. Grasshoppers also require a very large cage. One of the galvanized ash cans sold in supermarkets and hardware stores makes an ideal grasshopper "farm." The cover can be discarded in favor of a piece of screening, which will admit air and at the same time keep the frisky insects in place.

Grasshoppers like a lot of warmth. An interesting fact about grasshoppers of certain species is that they undergo a change of habit, and, indeed, of physiology, and turn into an entirely different creature. Not in appearance, but different in habit. This is the locust.

Many people think locusts and grasshoppers are different species of insects. The truth is that grasshoppers, usually a solitary insect, sometimes undergo a change which turns them into the gregarious locust, and then the individuals gather together, sometimes in huge swarms, overrunning the country, eating everything that grows as they travel. By the destruction of grain crops, such swarms of locusts have caused famines killing millions of people through starvation. The fight against

A long-horned grasshopper, one of the pretty common kind that are easy to raise.

locust hordes has been going on since several thousands of years before Christ and seems likely to continue for an indefinite time into the future.

Much study has been done on this strange transformation, and men have come to think that overcrowding is one of the main reasons grasshoppers turn into locusts. Food supplies for solitary grasshoppers need not be so abundant. While the appetite of the locust is insatiable, that of the solitary grasshopper is just average — for a hungry insect that is. Once the grasshoppers have become locusts, they feed incessantly, and eat everything that grows.

Grasshoppers are used as food for reptiles and small animals. Snakes and lizards particularly relish the succulent insects, as do birds and many other animals, including people — who eat them fried. Like crickets, grasshoppers drive their ovipositors deeply into the soil to lay their eggs in the fall, dying at the first frost. The young, hatching in the spring, never see their parents.

If you set up a grasshopper cage in one of the tall galvanized cans, you should put about three to six inches of clean, sifted soil in the bottom, dampening it slightly. A few rocks and several branchy plants can be stuck into the soil to provide supports for the insects to cling to. Feeding should be done in a wide, flat dish, such as a small pie plate. Any green leafy material will do, and household foods like lettuce, cabbage, celery, tomato — almost any vegetable — are good for the insects.

If you wish to raise grasshoppers, you will have to cage them a little differently than has just been described. Grasshoppers will lay eggs in cages if the proper conditions are provided. Keep your insects in an aquarium with a few sheets of newspaper on the bottom instead of soil. Toward the end of summer you must provide an egg-laying receptacle. This can be a small box of some kind, or a bowl of other deep dish. A bread pan is fine, too. The container should be filled with clean sand. As a matter of fact, unless you are certain that the sand is very clean, you should wash it, then bake it dry in the oven for two or three hours at about 350 degrees.

After the sand has cooled completely, it is placed into the box and sprinkled with warm water to dampen it thoroughly. Each day the sand must be sprinkled with enough water to keep it damp but not sopping wet. You may observe the grasshoppers laying eggs in the sand. If you do not actually see them perform this act, then you can examine the sand to see if the eggs are present. This should not be done until the sand has been in the cage for at least two weeks.

Sifted the sand through a large strainer. If the eggs are present, they will appear as small pods. If they are present, bury them in the sandbox once again and return the box to the cage, or place it in a warm, dry, dark location and replace it with a new box of sand in the cage to gather more eggs.

Some species of grasshoppers will hatch without a winter diapause. Others require this diapause before they hatch. If, within three or four weeks time, none of the eggs hatch, you may assume that the species you have requires the diapause, so you must give it to them in order to complete the cycle and effect a hatching.

Place the box of sand with the egg pods in it into the freezer for about twenty-four hours — long enough to make sure the sand and eggs have been frozen clear through. Now remove the box from the freezer and place it in an ordinary refrigerator for about one month. You should be able to find a spot near the back on one shelf of your regular house refrigerator to accommodate the small box.

Remove the box after a month, and, keeping the sand sprinkled as before — damp, but not wet — place it in a cage with a screen cover. The eggs should hatch in three to four weeks, and the young nymphs will immediately be able to feed on the same foods as the adults. Don't forget to put a water bottle in the cage with the nymphs.

CHAPTER TWELVE

Beetles

Having well over 300,000 different species to choose from, one would think it would be very easy to find many species of beetles which would make good insects to keep as pets. The truth is, going over available material, I have been hard put to select any specific one, mainly because of the difficulty of feeding them in captivity. True, there are beetles that eat everything, but to keep any particular species and find its food in an uninterrupted supply becomes so much of a burden that you will soon tire of the job. However, there are a couple of species that you can collect, observe for a time, then release.

If you want to go to some trouble, one species may be kept and even reared in a cage. This is the carrion beetle, or, as it is sometimes called, the burying beetle. These interesting and very pretty insects are the clean-up crews of our fields and woods. They are fairly common around farmyards, too, where an abundance of small animals, baby chicks, and other creatures may die and remain outside on the ground.

The carrion beetle will, upon discovering a dead mouse or chick, dig under the creature, removing the soil and steadily lowering the animal into the ground until it is entirely under the surface, then it will cover the carcass up. Now it will feed on the carcass and lay its eggs there so the larvae can also feed.

The mandibles of
this large beetle from
Guatemala are like
brushes, and enable
the insect to grasp
more securely.

A large aquarium with a glass cover can be used to rear
these beetles. You should put about six to eight inches of clean
loose soil in the bottom. Look around in the woods, field, or
barnyard for any small dead animal and lift it up to hunt for
your beetles. The beetles are large and colorful, having black
bodies with red bands across the abdomen, a red spot on the
head, and the red club-ends to the antennae. They are nearly ¾″
long. After you have found some — you will need several in
order to have them perform for you — they can be put in the
cage on top of the soil.

You may now either catch a mouse in a mousetrap and lay

this in the cage, or, if you haven't any mice in your house, look outside for a small dead animal that is not completely dried up, or, in a pinch, lay a small piece of meat on the soil. The meat should be raw, of course. The beetles will soon investigate the food, and, after satisfying themselves that it will do for their purpose, begin to bury it. A crew of industrious burying beetles can completely bury a creature the size of a small mouse or shrew in a few hours.

The most active of the burying beetles belong to the genus

A pair of these beetles can bury an animal like this field mouse in a few hours. It will provide food for the larvae after it has been entirely covered with soil.

Nicrophorus. Some of these beetles are selective in their choice of food, only liking small warm-blooded animals such as mice, birds, etc. Others prefer cold-blooded creatures such as small snakes, frogs, toads, and lizards. Your choice of food will depend upon where you find your original beetles.

Another kind of beetle that would be very interesting to watch, and which may perform for you in a cage, is the tumble-bug, or dung beetle. These belong to the genus *Canthon,* and they are one of the scarab beetles. Short, fat, and rounded, you can find one species in the summer on cow dung.

A pair of these strange little creatures will take bits of semisoft cow dung, pack it into a firm ball nearly twice as big as they are, then pushing industriously from behind, roll the ball quite a distance, finally digging a hole to bury it. Before the ball of dung is completely buried, the female will lay an egg in it. The larva, hatching, will feed upon the dung until it pupates within the ball to emerge as the adult beetle.

Since cow dung, even in its semisoft state, does not have an offensive odor, it is entirely reasonable to use it in a cage to observe the life history of the tumblebug.

Tumblebugs may be either dull black or dull green. They are small beetles, ⅜″ to ¾″ long, and nearly as broad. They are usually abundant on warmer days. The same conditions should be set up to keep them, except that the soil does not have to be as deep as for burying beetles. A small piece of the cow dung is all that is needed for the cage. Just make sure that the center of the cake is soft and moist.

The soil in both cages should be kept just damp enough to keep it from being dusty and powdery, but not wet. Either cage should be kept in a warm location — room temperature is fine — and out of the direct sunlight. The dung beetle will be able to stand temperatures warmer than the burying beetles.

CHAPTER THIRTEEN

Dragonflies

One of the most fascinating of all insects is the dragonfly. Before we go any further, let me tell you that all of the wild stories you may have heard about dragonflies are untrue. They do not sew up your lips, nor attack you, nor bite you or sting you with their tail. They are completely harmless to human beings. They are a terror to other flying insects, however, especially flies and mosquitos which they catch on the wing and devour while flying, the trapped victim held within a basket made by curving their legs around their prey. They belong to the order *Odonata*. There are a great number of species of these large and very beautiful creatures.

One thing this is so interesting is that their larvae are aquatic, but they are terrestrial. The young nymphs of dragonflies are hatched and live under water until the time to make their metamorphosis. At this time, the larva crawls up the stem of a water plant, reed, or stick, or, if it cannot find any of these supports standing out of the water, they crawl up the side of a rock or even onto the dirt bank of the stream.

Whatever support is provided, the larva climbs until it is well out of the water, then fastens itself securely by digging its feet into the object. Here it remains for a short time. Then, in a series of curious humping movements, it causes the skin to split

This dragonfly has nearly finished expanding its wings, after emerging from the dry shell of its larva.

right up the back. The larva itself is an ugly vicious-looking creature that has spent its entire existence crawling about in the mud at the bottom of a body of water. It emerges only to slash wickedly at a passing fish, tadpole, salamander, or other creature, grasping it in its extensible lower jaw and holding it securely with its strong mandibles while sucking it dry. From this lowly creature, the dragonfly emerges, pulling free after the skin has split, uncurling its long, slender abdomen, and pulling out the soft, rumpled wings.

Crawling up a little higher on the support, the dragonfly proceeds to expand its wings, then to fan them until they dry. As it does so, the wings take on a wonderful iridescence, or, in some species, a combination of actual color and iridescence. The bodies of many dragonflies are of brilliant metallic hues — gold, silver, red, green, blue — rainbow colors that flash in the sun as the lovely creature darts back and forth over a pond or stream looking for its food.

The adult dragonflies mate in the air while flying, and sail about holding each other close during the act. The female then lays her eggs. Most species lay them directly in the water, skimming the surface, then curving the abdomen down to just break the surface, laying their eggs which scatter and sink to the bottom. Some species pierce the stems of reeds and water plants below the surface of the water and lay their eggs within the plant tissues. When the young hatch, they crawl out of the stem and find refuge on the bottom in the mud.

The larvae of dragonflies spend the summer growing, and some overwinter by hibernating in the mud. In the spring they crawl out to make the change from monster to fairy creature.

An aquarium of about twenty-gallon size is fine for raising dragonflies. In this container place fine, washed sand or aquarium gravel to a depth of about two inches. On top of this, an inch-deep layer of sifted potting soil can be placed. Now fill the tank with water to about an inch or two from the top. Put a folded newspaper on the soil when you pour in the water, and pour slowly to keep from moving the soil and sand and mixing it too much. The water will become muddy when you fill the tank however careful you may be, so don't let this disturb you. Allow enough time for the water to settle and clear. This may be anywhere from a day to a week. Keep a cover glass on top to prohibit dust and other matter from falling into the water. Now you are ready for your larvae.

It is easy to catch dragonfly nymphs with a few simple tools. A piece of fly screening about 16″ x 24″ is your net. This should be tacked to two pieces of wood about one inch square and 16″ long. Have a jar to bring home your catch and a helper to go with you and you are all set for your expedition.

Select almost any small shallow stream which has a lot of rocks on the bottom. Stand downstream from your helper about two or three feet and place the end of the screen on the bottom, holding it slightly curved with the hollow facing your helper.

The author's son and a friend are catching dragonfly larvae. The screen is held down on the bottom while the rocks are lifted upstream.

Now have him suddenly lift rocks, roiling up the water as he does, and you catch all the debris he stirs up in your screen. As soon as the cloud of debris and mud has passed through the screen, lift it up and examine it. You will have everything from twigs and small pebbles to crayfish, worms, small fish, and, if you are lucky, a dragonfly larva or two. Dump these in the jar of water and rinse out the screen, then you are ready for another pass.

If you are careless in handling the larvae while catching them, they are very apt to catch you instead. The larvae can bite like a tiger! It is wise to pick them up with tweezers when

Examine the contents of the net as soon as all the muck has washed through it. Have a container ready to accept any catch.

This vicious-looking creature will turn into a lovely flying insect.

putting them into the jars and when transferring them to the tank at home.

If you collect several larvae and have a fair distance to go to get back home, it would be very wise to take several smaller jars with you, putting one larvae into each jar. This is to keep them from dining on each other along the way.

Another way that can be used to trap the larvae in still water is to use a strong screen sifter such as those found in kitchens. This should have a strong handle, and, if it does not, the handle should be reinforced by strapping a length of dowel to it, wrapping the dowel and handle together with strong cord, wire, or tape.

With this, wade into the pond a little way from the bank, then drag the sieve through the mud at the bottom, taking about half a sieveful at a stroke. Holding the strainer partly submerged, shake it gently from side to side to sift and wash out the mud. In the debris at the bottom you may find a larva or two. Sift over the bottom of the pond at different locations, and you are sure to come across some larvae at one place or another.

With the larvae established in your aquarium setup at home, the feeding is fairly simple. Simply put in several small guppies, a few tadpoles which you can find in the same pool you caught the larvae or other water creatures taken from the pool or stream. As long as you keep a supply of living creatures in the aquarium with the larvae, you need not worry about their feeding.

Of course, you will have to feed the guppies, if this is what you use. Don't feed them so heavily that the water is fouled, though. The other water creatures will probably feed upon each other, so you will have no trouble there. The only thing you will have to watch is that there are always some left for the dragonfly larvae.

From about the middle to the end of summer — when you see the larvae reaching a length of an inch or more — place several small straight twigs in the tank so they reach up out of the water after being stuck down through the mud clear to the bottom. The larvae cannot crawl up the slippery glass, and, unless you provide them with supports on which to climb up out of the water, they will drown. This sounds strange, that a water creature will drown, but at the time of metamorphosis, the breathing apparatus of the insect changes from gills for using water into lungs for using air, and this changeover is a critical time for the creature.

You will have the problem of the dragonflies being free in the room after they metamorphose. This can be solved by either making a tall cage out of screening and inverting this over the entire aquarium, leaving enough room at the top for your twigs, or by using some other kind of container, perhaps like the coffee-can brooder illustrated in chapter five into which the twig with the larva on it can be lifted from the aquarium after the larva has fastened itself in place, and inserted into the brooder, where the dragonfly will remain trapped after it has dried its wings. Be sure that the twigs are not moved until the larva is well fastened, or it may drop off. If this is the case, it may very well be unable to refasten itself before the splitting of the skin occurs, and the insect will be unable to transform properly. You might even wait until the dragonfly has pulled itself from the case of the larva, *then* move the twig, since the insect will not fly until the wings have been expanded and dried.

It would be very difficult if not impossible to effect a mating of the adult dragonflies, since, as described earlier, they mate on the wing, in full and bright sunlight, then must have a large body of water to fly over to lay the eggs. The adults may be mounted as specimens in your "bug" collection, or, better still, released outdoors where they will find their place over water and be able to complete their destiny unharmed.

Different larvae, taken from different ponds, may produce dragonflies of different species and colors, each more beautiful than the one before. You may like to try to raise all the kinds found in your section of the country.

CHAPTER FOURTEEN

Insect Collections

It might be a good idea to tell you how to mount different insects, so if you want to make a collection for school or study, you will at least know how to start properly. Too many "collections" are really only accumulations so poorly mounted and so incorrectly catalogued that all they amount to is a bunch of dead bugs, most of them damaged in one way or another.

This is not to say that young people shouldn't collect insects, but only that most young people, having an interest in making a collection, do not know how to go about it, and there isn't a great deal written for students or youngsters about preparation. But don't be too saddened about this. I have known several school science teachers who should have been ashamed of the way they mounted specimens they used for study in the classroom. A really good insect mounter is hard to come by, and they are in demand in museums and universities to take care of the study collections.

Butterflies and moths are mounted in the same fashion. This is a different way than beetles, flies, and other insects are mounted. In mounting *lepidoptera* (butterflies and moths), care must be taken not to smudge the wings and rub off the scales. This happens if you do not handle the insect in a proper manner. Still, considerable handling can be done without damaging the wings if you do it properly.

To begin with, a moth or butterfly cannot be mounted if it is not soft and pliable. This is called relaxed, and to relax a butterfly you must subject it to high humidity, to permit the muscles and body parts to soak up moisture. Of course, if you catch a moth, or have one emerge from the cocoon and mount it before it dries out, so much the better, and you do not have to go through the relaxing procedure. But let us suppose that the specimens you will be mounting have been killed and papered for some time. A butterfly or moth, properly papered, can be set aside for a great many years, then be relaxed and spread, and it will be in perfect condition, showing no sign of deterioration at all. Not too long ago I spread a small moth from Germany for my own collection. The date on the paper it was stored in was 1891 — more than eighty years ago. Not a scale was disturbed on the wings.

To relax insects you need a small waterproof box which can be tightly closed. Into the bottom of this box pour about one inch of clean sand. Now cut a piece of screening to fit inside on top of the sand after both ends have been bent down to form legs to keep the screening propped up off the surface of the sand. This trivet is to keep the insects being relaxed from absorbing too much water. The sand should be saturated with water until the surface shows wet. A few drops of disinfectant such as Lysol can be added to the sand in order to inhibit the growth of fungus. The insects are placed on the screen, separated from each other, and the box closed and put aside for a day.

For lepidoptera you need a device called a spreading board. These may be purchased, or you can make your own. Two pieces of model airplane balsawood, about 4″ wide, ¼″ thick, and 10″ long, and a strip of cork, about ½″ thick, 2″ wide and 10″ long, will make an excellent board. With model cement, glue both sheets of balsa to the strip of cork (if you cannot find cork, a third piece of balsa the same size will do) so that there is a gutter between the balsa about ½″ wide. This means that each sheet of balsa will overlap the edge of the cork strip ¾″. This will be enough to support the balsa. The gully or gutter is to accommodate the bodies of the butterflies while they are drying.

Having obtained a spreading board, the first thing to do is to fasten a strip of tracing cloth or paper to each side of the groove. This can be with thumbtacks or a length of masking tape. The strips should lie right along the groove, not more than

Paper or tracing-cloth strips should be fastened to the board on each side of the body groove.

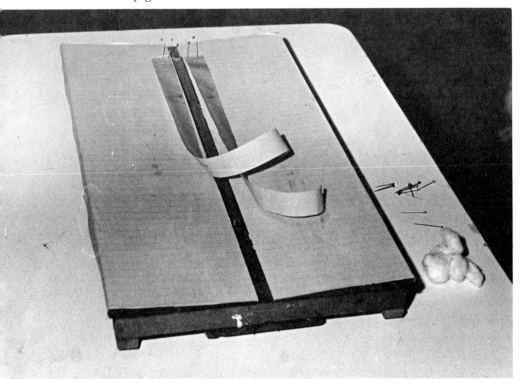

1/16″ away. They should be about ½″ wide. Leave them loose at one end. Now take an insect from the relaxing box, and, grasping it by the body, blow in between the wings. If they separate readily, the insect is relaxed enough to spread.

You will need insect pins for mounting. These are purchased in hobby stores, school supply and biological supply houses, and come in several sizes. Thin ones are used for small-bodied insects and heavier ones for larger bodies. Select a pin that is suitable for the insect you are spreading, and, still holding it firmly by the body, slip the pin straight down through the center of the thorax. (The thorax is the part of the insect right behind the head and corresponds to your own chest.) The pin should be centered carefully on the thorax and should project through the body of the insect about ½″. Blow between the

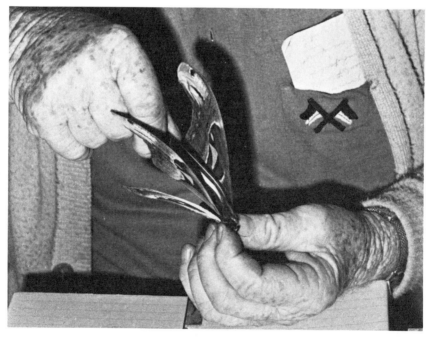

The body is firmly grasped between the thumb and forefinger, and a pin, held in rigid tweezers, is pushed vertically through the thorax.

wings as you push in the pin, to keep them spread apart, and avoid rubbing off any scales.

Do not let go of the pin when it is through, but now, releasing the body of the insect, carry it by the pin to the spreading board and stick it in the groove on the board, pushing the pin down until the wing joints are even with the surface at the sides of the groove. For smaller specimens, and even for the large ones, it may be easier to use tweezers to hold the pin. There will be less likelihood of harming the specimen if you do.

You will need a setting needle for the next operation. This is just a stiff sharp needle, pushed into a short length of dowel

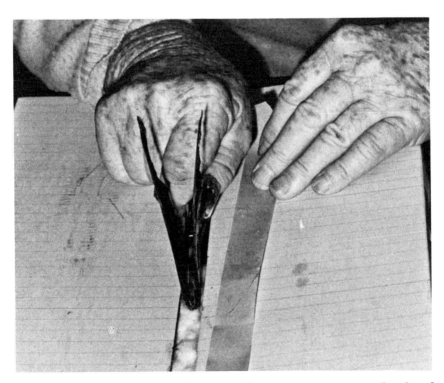

The specimen, still held by the pin in the tweezer, is accurately placed in the groove of the spreading board. Push the pin down until the wing joints are just at the surface of the board.

or balsawood strip. The eye end is pushed into the wood, leaving the point for you to work with. Lift one strip of paper on the board, then, using this setting needle, push down one wing until it lies flat on the board, letting the strip fall back in place over the wing to hold it flat. Stick a pin through the end of the

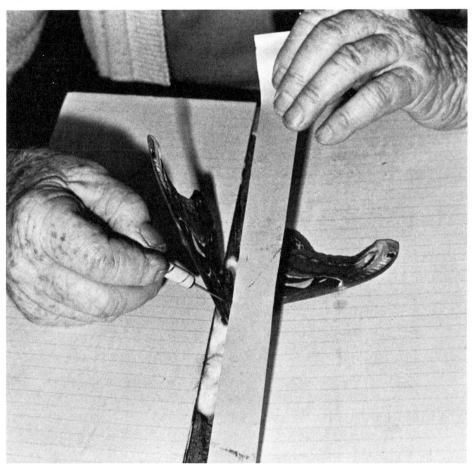

With the setting needle, press one wing down and pull the strip over it to hold it flat.

strip after pulling it taut over the wing. Repeat this operation with the other wing.

Now, placing the point of the setting needle just behind the *costa* — the large stiff vein at the leading edge of the wing — of the forewing, and close to the body, push the wing up until

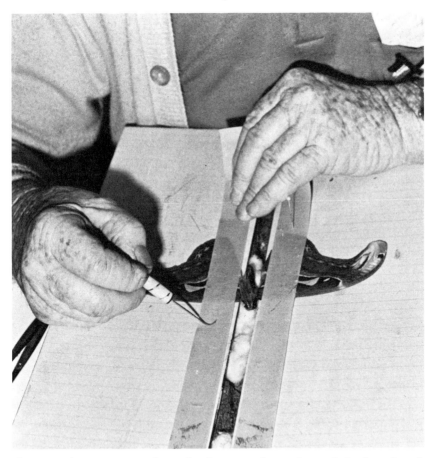

The second wing is now brought down to the surface of the board and held in place with the strip. A pin is stuck through each strip to keep it in place.

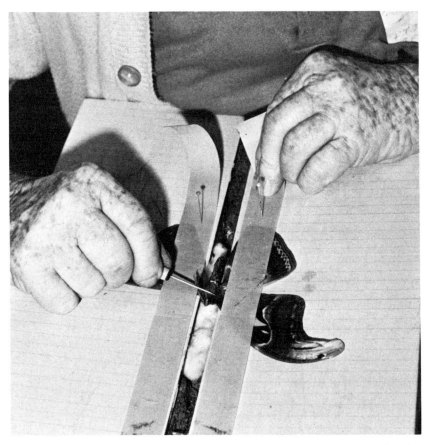

The forewing is pushed up until the rear edge is exactly perpendicular to the body. The setting needle is used close to the costa and the body.

the rear edge is exactly perpendicular to the body. That is at right angles to it. It is at this point where most beginners make their mistake. The *rear* edges of the front wings *must* make a perfectly straight line right across the body, and the body *must* be at right angles to both front wings. If this is not done, the insect will look drooping and unsightly.

In order to push the wing, you may or may not have to lift the paper strip holding the wing just enough to loosen the wing for the movement. If this is the case, when the wing is in position, place a fingertip on the strip and press down on the wing to keep it from slipping. Still holding the wing in place, put a

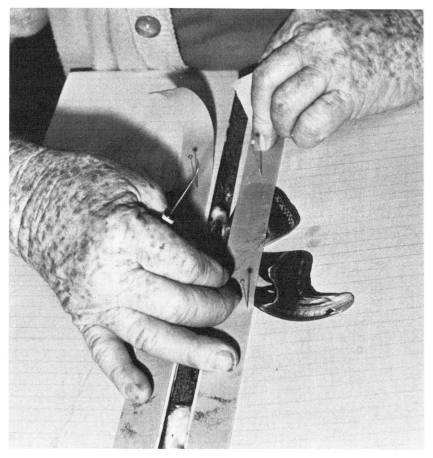

Two pins are put through the strip as close to the costa as possible to keep pressure on the wings so that it does not slip back.

pin through the tape right next to the front edge of the wing but not through it. Two pins are used if the specimen is large.

The hind wings must now be pulled up into position. It is difficult to say exactly how high to pull the hind wings, because this will vary slightly with each species. Generally, when the center of the *leading* edge of the hind wing is at a point one third of the way in from the outside on the *trailing* edge of the front wing, the pattern on the wings of the insect fall into a natural sequence. The hind wings must be *under* the front wings.

Since the hind wings lack the heavy and strong costa of the front wings, more care must be taken with the needle not to tear the fragile wing. Stay very close to the body while pulling. Pins are pushed through the strip at the edges of the hind wings to hold them in place, and small strips of glass may be dropped onto the tips of the wings to flatten them and to keep them from curling as the insect dries. For easier handling, a

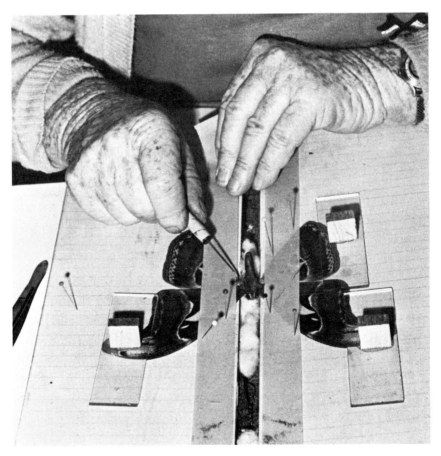

In setting the hind wings, be very gentle, because they do not have the stiff costa to keep them from tearing. Stay very close to the body and to the front edge of the wing.

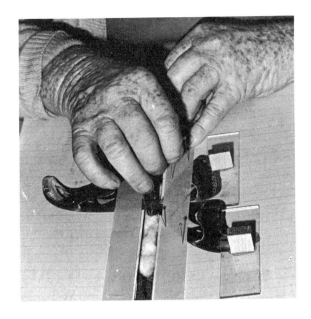

Pins are now set through the strip at the hind wings to hold them firmly in place.

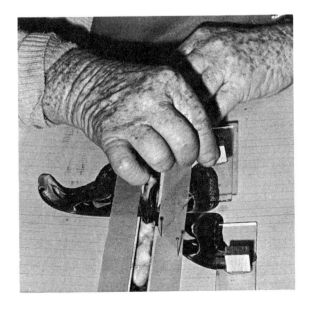

A small strip of glass is now dropped onto the wing tips to keep them in place, and to keep them from curling as the insect dries on the board.

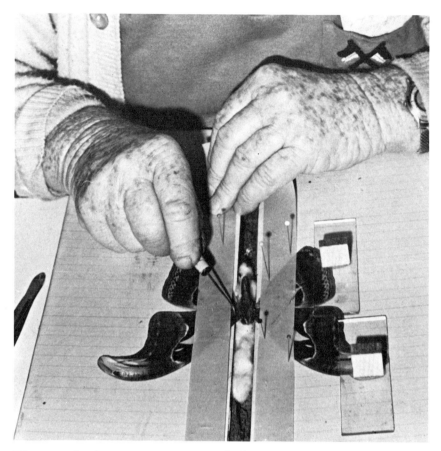

The second side is set in position as before.

small piece of balsawood may be cemented to one side of the glass strips to provide a handle.

The second side of the butterfly is now spread as before. After the wings are all set, the pins and the glass strips in place, you can work on the head and antennae. A small piece of cotton, placed in the groove, is pulled up under the head, permitting some cotton to stick out in front of the head to support the antennae. The antennae are teased into position with the setting

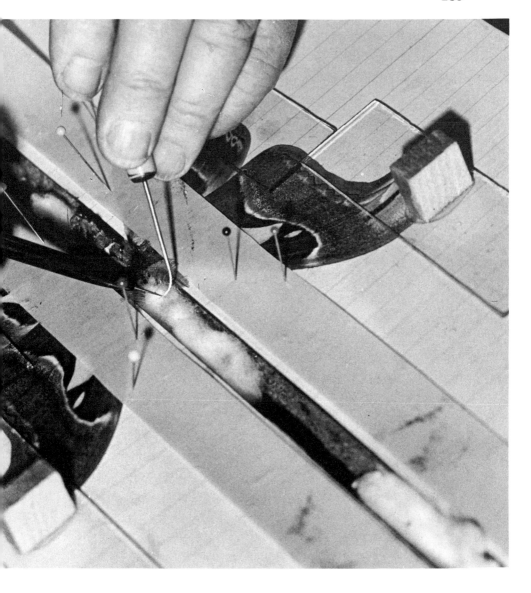

After the wings are set and the pins and glass are in place, cotton is pulled up to the head of the insect to support the antennae.

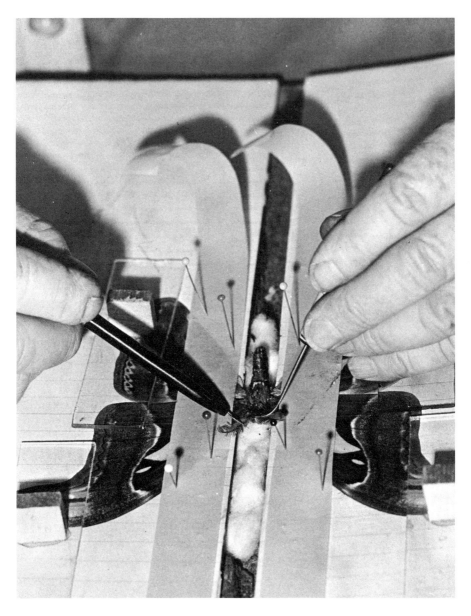

The antennae are teased into an approximate position with two setting needles.

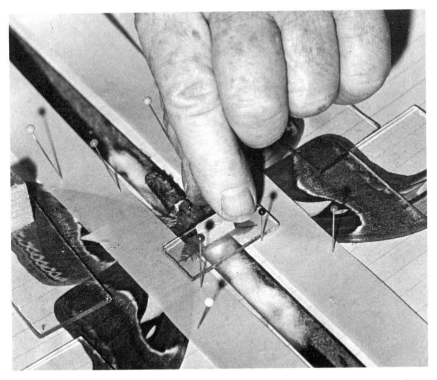

The antennae can be flattened in place with a short glass, after they have been pulled into position and combed out with the setting needles. The completed specimen is now ready to dry for several days before removal from the board.

needle. It will be easier if you use two needles at this point, one to hold the antenna in place and the other, if the antenna is feathery as on a moth, to comb out the feathers and generally smooth them down. Another small wafer of glass may be dropped over the antennae to hold them in position and keep them flat. If necessary, the rear end of the body may also be propped up with a piece of cotton pushed in place with a setting needle. This is necessary when the body curls as the insect dries.

The finished specimen may be put in a safe place to dry, before removing it from the spreading board.

The finished specimen is put in a safe place to dry for a few days, after which time it may be removed from the board, leaving the pin through the thorax, since this is the pin by which the specimen is fastened in the collection box. If care is taken to position the first insect high up on the spreading board, more than one may be spread on the same board. Be sure to leave room btween the specimens for the front wings to push up to their proper position. For very small butterflies or moths, smaller boards may be made, leaving only a ¼" groove between the balsawood sheets. If the groove is too wide, the insect will be suspended by the tips of its wings, with no support for the body.

Beetles and other insects are mounted differently from butterflies. Beetles are not usually spread, although sometimes one side — the left — is spread, lifting the *elytra* (wing cover) up in the flight position, and spreading the left wings. The pin is placed through the right-wing cover, centered about one third of the way back toward the tail, in beetles. Other insects have the pin pushed through the rear of the thorax, centered on the right side. This goes for crickets, grasshoppers, bees, and bugs.

Extremely small insects are usually mounted on points. These are cardboard or plastic wedge-shaped points which are mounted on a pin pushed through the large end of the point, and the insect is fixed to the pointed end by a small bit of adhesive. Punches can be purchased which punch out points from card stock.

All insects should be mounted by their pins in specimen boxes. These are obtainable from the same places as pins and other entomological supplies, and come in a variety of sizes and prices, from very low-priced cardboard boxes with glass tops, to elaborate cabinets wherein the boxes are drawers. Beneath each insect should be a label, giving the name of the specimen, where and when it was caught, or, if you raised it, put an X in front of the stage you began with — i.e., X-ova; X-larva, X-pupa, etc. The name of the collector should also be placed on the label. Also the date should be listed.

A collection without pertinent information is useless for study purposes. It can only be looked at as something pretty, but it tells you nothing unless careful and accurate data is supplied.

Whatever kind of specimen box you use to house your collection, the mounted insects should be protected against invasion by other insects, and by small spiders. These have the unhappy habit of eating the bodies of the preserved insects, letting the wings fall to the bottom of the case. Protection is easy. You may secure a moth ball in the lower right-hand corner of the case by crossing two pins in front of the moth ball, holding it against the corner sides of the container. You may, with a spot of white glue or epoxy, fasten a small plastic box in the same place — the lower right-hand corner, then fill it with paradichlorobenzene flakes. If the box has a cover, this should be perforated with several small holes drilled through to permit the gas from the disinfectant to permeate the specimen case. Both the moth balls and the flakes should be renewed every few months as they dissipate, and an inspection each three months or so will keep check of this for you.

Index